THE LAW OF POLICING

FEDERAL CONSTITUTIONAL PRINCIPLES

by Randy Means

LRIS PUBLICATIONS
PORTLAND, OREGON

Published by Labor Relations Information System
3021 NE Broadway
Portland OR 97232
503.282.5440
www.LRIS.com

Means, Randolph B. 1949 -

ISBN 978-1-880607-23-7

Library of Congress Control No. 2007921274

Cover design by Marc R. Fuller

DEDICATION

On the day a law enforcement officer takes the oath of office the Constitution becomes more than a legal obligation – it becomes a matter of promise keeping. This book is dedicated to the countless law enforcement officers who work hard to keep faith with their oaths of office. In particular, it is dedicated to those noble officers who see the Constitution not as an obstacle on their professional pathway, but as the pathway itself.

Respectfully,
Randy Means

ACKNOWLEDGMENTS

First, to my wife Katherine I extend my heartfelt thanks for her work and patience in helping me assemble these thoughts. Her help was instrumental in allowing me to complete this undertaking.

I thank Will Aitchison, Debbie Frields, Marc Fuller, Kristin Winges, and Carol Green of Labor Relations Information System – all of whom were involved in the preparation of this book – for their professionalism and kindness.

I also thank Professors Arnold Loewy and William Murphy who taught me constitutional law and criminal procedure at the University of North Carolina School of Law more than 30 years ago. They were wonderful teachers and I made As in their classes. Their work caused my original interest in this subject matter and I am grateful.

I thank my friend and teacher Dennis Andrade, career criminal investigator, who for more than 20 years patiently showed me what good police work looks like.

When I first attended FBI Academy training for police legal advisers a quarter of a century ago, I was taught the subjects of which I now write. My instructors were Dan Schofield and John Hall. They provided great models of police legal training and I thank them.

Most importantly, I thank my three career-long mentors, Reece Trimmer, Bob Farb, and Bob Thomas. Their thinking has so affected mine over the years that today I am unable to tell exactly where theirs ends and mine begins.

Reece Trimmer is a Harvard Law School graduate who himself has taught at a fine law school and who has devoted nearly four decades to the police legal field. In my world, he is the Dean of the school of police law. He was my first mentor and surely some of my words here were originally his.

Bob Farb, also a Harvard-educated attorney, is today a long-tenured Professor of Public Law and Government at the University of North Carolina. For 26 years, I have studied his books on police law. Today, I am proud to say that, at his request, I review his police law texts prior to their publication in order to add occasional, if unspectacular, insights.

To my law partner, Bob Thomas, I reserve my greatest thanks. A leader in the police law profession since the mid-70s, he is recognized by many, including me, as perhaps the best police legal analyst in the United States. A Phi Beta Kappa graduate of the University of North Carolina, where he also received his Juris Doctor degree, he has headed the national association of law enforcement legal advisors (IACP-LOS), served as counsel to the American Society of Law Enforcement Trainers (ASLET), and was litigation manager in *Graham v. Connor*, the landmark decision of the United States Supreme Court on use of force by police. He was for many years the Senior Attorney for the Charlotte Police Department and later served as Counsel to the Mecklenburg County Sheriff's Office, also in Charlotte. My work and his have been so intertwined for 25 years that I am certain I have borrowed many of his thoughts and, occasionally, his phrases. I have made no effort to purge my words of his. At this point it would be too difficult and, if done thoroughly, no doubt would strip this writing of some of its best.

For any wisdom in this book I acknowledge and thank my mentors. Errors are mine.

Randy Means

ABOUT THE AUTHOR

Randy Means, a partner in the Charlotte, North Carolina, based law firm of Thomas and Means, L.L.P., specializes entirely in police operations and administration and assists a broad national clientele. He is the primary legal and risk management instructor for the International Association of Chiefs of Police, senior legal instructor and consultant for the Institute of Police Technology and Management, and teaches regularly in a number of police leadership academies and command colleges. His work has been mentioned in the "Wall Street Journal" and discussed on "60 Minutes". He has appeared on both the Law Enforcement Television Network and the FBI Training Network.

He has been a speaker at national annual conferences of the FBI National Academy Alumni Association (FBINAA), Southern Police Institute (SPI) Alumni Association, International Association of Chiefs of Police (IACP), Public Risk and Insurance Management Association (PRIMA), State Risk Manager's Association (STRIMA), Public Agency Risk Manager's Association (PARMA), National Association of State Personnel Executives (NASPE), National Association of Government Training and Development Directors (NAGTADD) International Association of State Directors of Law Enforcement Standards and Training (IASDLEST), International Personnel Management Association (IPMA), National Association of Field Training Officers (NAFTO), National Intelligence Academy (NIA), International Association of Law Enforcement Planners (IALEP), American Society for Law Enforcement Training (ASLET), Labor Relations Information System (LRIS), International Association of Arson Investigators, North American Wildlife Enforcement Officers Association, National Information Officers Association (NIOA), National Conference of State and Provincial Police Planning Officers, Mid-Atlantic Law Enforcement Executive Development (LEED) Conference, the California Association of Police Training Officers (CAPTO), and COPSWEST (California Peace Officers Association), as well as annual police chiefs and sheriffs conferences in many states. He has taught for the British Columbia Police Complaint Commission, the Los Angeles County Police Chiefs Association, Northwestern University, the Southwestern Law Enforcement

Institute and is a member of the adjunct faculty of the University of North Florida.

He has done law enforcement training in 47 states and specialized, in-house liability management training for the Los Angeles County Sheriff's Department, the San Diego County Sheriff's Department, the Phoenix Police Department, the Honolulu Police Department, the Las Vegas Metropolitan Police Department, the Tucson Police Department, the Detroit Police Department, the Oregon State Police, the Alaska State Troopers, Arizona POST, California POST, Nevada POST, the Colorado State Police, the New Jersey State Police, the Kansas Highway Patrol, the North Carolina Highway Patrol, the Utah Highway Patrol, the St. Louis County Police Department, the Fairfax County (VA) Police Department, the Florida Marine Patrol, the United States Park Police, and the Drug Enforcement Administration (DEA), among hundreds of others. He has conducted law enforcement and risk management training for dozens of insurance and risk management companies and pools from coast to coast and for hundreds of academies and other institutional providers of law enforcement training.

A graduate of the University of North Carolina School of Law, he formerly served as head of legal training for North Carolina's state law enforcement training center, coordinator of legal training for the North Carolina State Bureau of Investigation, and Police Attorney for the City of Charlotte. He currently serves on the Board of Directors of the National Association of Police Legal Advisors (IACP-LOS), manages the "Chief's Counsel" column for "Police Chief" magazine, and writes the legal column for "Law and Order" magazine. He has trained nearly a quarter-million law enforcement officials in his almost three decades of service to the law enforcement community.

PREFACE

This writing is no substitute for a scholarly treatise. It is certainly not comprehensive. Rather, it is intended as a comparatively short, easy-to-read guide to its subject matter. Its primary use may be by law enforcement officers and those who teach the law of policing and related liability. To the extent that it serves the many attorneys and others who seek to navigate these waters, that secondary benefit is welcome.

Because case discussions and citations may hinder the flow of reading and since any comprehensive research should be performed with benefit of treatises and computers in any event, case law coverage in this book is limited almost entirely to representative decisions of the United States Supreme Court and the federal courts of appeals. There are 13 federal courts of appeal. Twelve of them have geographical areas of responsibility and decide criminal and civil rights cases. A decision of such a federal appeals court is binding law only in the geographical area over which that court has jurisdiction. In other parts of the country, such a decision would be studied for its possible persuasive value. For the many who have not memorized the boundaries of the various federal circuits, a map is provided below.

Geographic Boundaries Of United States Courts of Appeals and United States District Courts

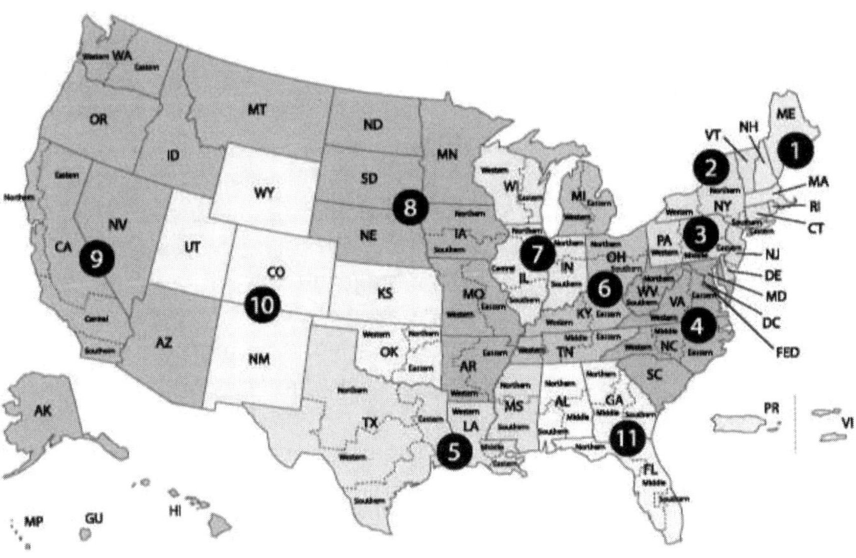

State appellate court decisions are far too numerous and varied to be approached meaningfully in this writing and, for several reasons, sometimes provide poor guidance on federal constitutional principles. Naturally, a state appeals court decision is of great concern to those in that state. Thankfully, there are writings in most states that put forward the state-based statutory and case law that must be considered in reaching appropriate policy and procedure. Advice of local counsel, ideally expert in police legal matters, is essential.

Hopefully, this book will be read by many non-lawyers. Because it contains hundreds of case citations, those uninitiated in legal research may want to know that a case citation refers first to the volume number in which a particular publisher places a case decision. Next, the publisher and possibly the series of the publication are identified. Third is the page number at which the case is found in the referenced volume. Last, in parentheses, is the year in which the decision was rendered and, in the case of a federal appeals court decision, its circuit number. (e.g., *United States v. McKoy*, 428 F.3d 38 (1st Cir. 2005)). Throughout this book, a variety of citations to published authorities has been used. To assist you in locating these authorities, the following glossary provides the full names of publications which may have been referred to in the book. If you have difficulties locating a particular case, please contact Labor Relations Information System for information on how to find it. Use of computers in legal research may eliminate the need to actually handle the sometimes dusty books.

Abbreviation	Full Name
F.2d	Federal Reporter, Second Series
F.3d	Federal Reporter, Third Series
F. Supp.	Federal Supplement
F. Supp.2d	Federal Supplement, Third Series
F. Supp.3d	Federal Supplement, Third Series
S.Ct.	Supreme Court Reporter
U.S.	United States Reporter

WARNING

This writing is based on federal law. There may be state law in your jurisdiction that is more restrictive of police procedure and/or more expansive of police liability than is federal law. Advice of local legal counsel is essential and is recommeded with respect to all matters discussed in this writing. No action, policy, or procedure should be undertaken solely in reliance on this publication.

TABLE OF CONTENTS

CHAPTER 4

CHAPTER 6

CHAPTER 7

CHAPTER 9

CHAPTER 10

CHAPTER 11

CHAPTER 12

CHAPTER 1

INTRODUCTION AND DEFINITIONS

Naturally, it is critical that law enforcement officers know and follow the law. It would be ironic indeed if law enforcement work were to begin by law violation. Law **enforcement,** then, is reason in itself for law enforcement officers to obey the law, most importantly, the supreme law of the land – the United States Constitution. The oath of office is another positive reason for police to remain mindful of the law. Most oaths of office involve promises that officers will "support, uphold and defend" the Constitution of the United States of America. Surely in that lofty promise there is a necessarily implied sub-promise – that officers themselves will not become knowing violators of the very instrument that they have so solemnly pledged to support, uphold and defend.

Beyond these positive reasons to obey the Constitution, there are several negative ones. It is a federal felony for a law enforcement officer to willfully violate the Constitution. Also, officers may be sued civilly for constitutional rights violations. Of course, there is the threat of evidence exclusion. Evidence which is the direct product of a violation of someone's constitutional rights cannot be used, in a criminal prosecution, against the person whose rights were violated. The suppression of such evidence is required by what is now known as the "exclusionary rule" or "fruit of the poisoned tree" doctrine. Last, and as might be expected given the matters explained above, law enforcement employers may take administrative disciplinary action against an officer who violates constitutional rights. So, for a variety of reasons positive and negative, it is imperative that officers keep up with the law, especially obligations created by the federal Constitution.

While some state law is more restrictive of police behavior than is the federal Constitution, most of it is a mirror image of federal principles.

This book examines certain aspects of what some lawyers would call "pre-arraignment criminal procedure," the law of criminal investigation and, in particular, what law enforcement officers can and cannot do under the United States Constitution. While some state law is more restrictive of police behavior than is the federal Constitution, most of it is a mirror image of federal principles. In fact, much state statutory law in this area is an outgrowth of the "Model Code of Pre-Arraignment Criminal Procedure," which was born in the mid-1970s and was intended largely to guide state law onto pathways that would not offend emerging federal Constitutional principles. State law may be more restrictive of police practices than the federal Constitution but naturally it cannot be more permissive. State law that purports to be more permissive than the federal Constitution is by definition unconstitutional. The starting point, then, in determining the legality of a police action is deciding whether it passes muster under the federal Constitution. This book is devoted to exactly that. While some of this book studies interrogation practices and identification procedures, most of it deals with interpretation of the Fourth Amendment to the United States Constitution – the law of "search and seizure." Consequently, it begins with definitions of those two terms, as used in Fourth Amendment constitutional law.

State law may be more restrictive of police practices than the federal Constitution but naturally it cannot be more permissive.

What Is A "Search"?

A search occurs whenever a law enforcement officer intrudes upon a reasonable expectation of privacy. Such "intrusions" may or may not be "physical." Merely looking in a window of a home is a search if it "intrudes" upon a reasonable privacy expectation. Secretly listening to or recording a conversation in which there is a reasonable expectation of privacy is a search. Certain electronic activities may intrude upon reasonable privacy expectations. If an officer walks by a car that is in a public place and looks into the car through the window, he has not conducted a search; a person cannot reasonably expect privacy in what he knowingly exposes to public view. On the other hand, if an officer opens the trunk of a car and merely looks into the trunk, a search has occurred because the officer intruded into a zone where privacy can reasonably be expected. The fact that the officer did not touch or move any item in the trunk is irrelevant. Once the officer has intruded upon a reasonable expectation of privacy, he has conducted a search. Unless a valid consent has been obtained, a search must be justified either by a search warrant or some recognized exception to the search warrant requirement.

What Is A "Seizure"?

A seizure of a person occurs whenever a law enforcement officer uses force on someone or a person submits to an officer's "show of authority." When an officer says or does things that would cause a reasonable person to feel that he or she is required to participate in a contact with the officer, that person has been "seized." So if a uniformed officer approaches someone on a sidewalk and says "Hold up there...I need to talk to you," a reasonable person would feel he was being required to stop. Assuming he does stop (submits), as instructed, a seizure has occurred. The constitutional implications of seizing someone are discussed in detail later.

A seizure of property occurs when an officer interferes meaningfully or significantly with another person's possessory interest in that property. Requiring that someone hand over a weapon during a brief detention is not a seizure of constitutional implication because the "interference" with a "possessory interest" is not so significant as to invoke the Fourth Amendment. However, a non-consensual "pat-down" which might reveal the presence of that weapon would be a search, as explained above, and would require Fourth Amendment justification. Taking that same weapon (non-consensually) to the police department for "safekeeping" or for processing would be a seizure which also would require satisfaction of the Fourth Amendment requirement that searches and seizures be reasonable.

United States v. Jacobsen, 466 U.S.109 (1984) provides a good summary and discussion of the above-stated definitions.

The Fourth Amendment prohibits "unreasonable" searches and seizures.

"Unreasonableness" And Its Consequences

The Fourth Amendment prohibits "unreasonable" searches and seizures. To be reasonable, searches and seizures must be justified by facts and/or circumstances suggesting the need for them – probable cause, for example. Without such justification, searches and seizures are unreasonable and therefore unconstitutional. Consequently, as stated above, any evidence which is the direct product of a violation of someone's constitutional rights is inadmissible in a criminal prosecution of the person whose rights were violated. An officer who intentionally violates someone's constitutional rights is guilty of a federal felony. Civil lawsuits against police for alleged constitutional rights violations are now commonplace.

Civil lawsuits against police for alleged constitutional rights violations are now commonplace.

This book contains hundreds of examples of what federal courts find to be reasonable, and unreasonable, searches and seizures. In other portions of this book are discussions of the law of interview and interrogation – the *Miranda* Rule and interpretations of the Fifth and Sixth Amendments. It begins with the law of officer-citizen contacts, seizures and non-seizures of persons.

CHAPTER 2

SEIZURES AND NON-SEIZURES OF PERSONS – VOLUNTARY CONTACTS, INVESTIGATIVE DETENTIONS, AND ARRESTS

Determining the reasonableness of a seizure involves balancing the individual's right to be free and left alone by police with the occasional need of law enforcement to interfere with privacy and freedom in order to investigate crime and enforce laws.

The Fourth Amendment to the United States Constitution requires that all searches and seizures, including seizures of persons, be reasonable. Determining the reasonableness of a seizure involves balancing the individual's right to be free and left alone by police with the occasional need of law enforcement to interfere with privacy and freedom in order to investigate crime and enforce laws. Following is an examination of the legal concepts involved in officer-citizen contacts, including seizures of persons.

For purposes of federal constitutional law, officer-citizen contacts fall into one of three legal categories:

1. Voluntary Contacts.
2. Investigative Detentions ("Terry Stops").
3. Arrests.

Investigative detentions and arrests are "seizures"; voluntary contacts are not.

Courts may use different words to describe these transactions but, ultimately, there are only three categories. Officers are required to control a contact so that it does not escalate into an intrusion (seizure) for which the officer may not have legal justification. Before it can be determined what legal justification, if any, is required for an officer-citizen contact, it is necessary to determine what type of contact is taking place. In order to do that, one must know the characteristics of each type of contact.

Before it can be determined what legal justification, if any, is required for an officer-citizen contact, it is necessary to determine what type of contact is taking place.

The Voluntary Contact

Where there is no "seizure" within the meaning of the Fourth Amendment, there is no Fourth Amendment requirement of "reasonable" factual justification for the contact. In a voluntary contact, because there is no seizure, police need not have or prove reasonable suspicion or probable cause. For that reason, among several other practical advantages, voluntary contacts tend to serve well the interests of police.

The "Objective" Test As To Whether A Contact Is Voluntary

Officer-citizen contacts are legally voluntary if, in view of all circumstances surrounding the transaction, a reasonable person would have believed he was free to leave and/or decline the contact with law enforcement officers. This test focuses on what officers have actually said and/or done, and how reasonable people would interpret those words and actions. According to the Supreme Court, "Only when the officer, by means of physical force or show of authority, has restrained the liberty of a citizen may we conclude that a 'seizure' has occurred." *California v. Hodari D*, 499 U.S. 621 (1991).

"Only when the officer, by means of physical force or show of authority, has restrained the liberty of a citizen may we conclude that a 'seizure' has occurred."

The test for seizure of a person involves an objective standard – looking to a reasonable person's interpretation of police behavior rather than to the suspect's personal (subjective) view of it. This standard ensures that the scope of an officer's Fourth Amendment authority does not vary with the state of mind of the particular individual approached by the officer. In *Florida v. Bostick*, 501 U.S. 429 (1991), the Supreme Court specified that the reasonable person is an innocent person and therefore presumably does not suffer guilt-induced paranoia every time police approach. An individual suspect may feel and may testify that he was detained or arrested at a given point in time, but unless the officer has said or done something that would cause a reasonable person to feel that way, no seizure has occurred. See, for example, *United States v. Al Nasser,* 479 F.3d 1166 (9th Cir. 2007).

Whether the involved officer himself subjectively believed he was or was not seizing someone – and, if so, whether he was arresting or merely detaining him – is generally not relevant to the legal determination. An officer may believe that his action in seizing a person was only a detention, but a court may still decide that the objective facts showed that the officer's action was an arrest and therefore required probable cause.

Free To Leave Versus Free To Decline

Some have suggested that whether an officer-citizen contact amounts to a seizure depends upon whether the citizen is free to leave. This is a bit of an overstatement. While a "free to leave" inquiry is often determinative, it is not the sole test for whether an officer-citizen contact is a seizure. There are circumstances in which someone is not necessarily free to leave but the contact still may be voluntary in the legal sense.

For example: Suppose in an attempted armed robbery of a convenience store clerk, the clerk and gunman scuffle. The perpetrator fires but only wounds himself. He flees but police find his blood and obtain his physical description. Thirty minutes later, police learn that a person has arrived at a nearby hospital with a gunshot wound; he matches the description of the robbery suspect. Police go to the hospital and obtain permission from the emergency room doctor to speak with the suspect while he is awaiting treatment in an examination room. The doctor tells police that the subject has not received any medication and that his wound is superficial. There ensues the following conversation with the suspect:

> Officer: "Good afternoon. I'm Officer John Smith with the City Police Department. How are you feeling?"
>
> Suspect: "O.K. A few stitches and I'll be as good as new."
>
> Officer: "Great. Sir, may I have your permission to talk with you a moment? Would you allow me to do that?"
>
> Suspect: "Sure. No problem. What's up?"

The "free to decline" test has been applied by the United States Supreme Court in several cases.

In this scenario, the suspect arguably was not free to leave in that he was waiting in a hospital to receive treatment for his injury. Still, it appears he was free to decline the contact with the officer. Nothing in the officer's communication indicated otherwise. He asked the suspect to participate in the transaction; there were no words of command, demand, requirement, or instruction. Though the suspect may not have been "free to leave," circumstances indicated he was "free to decline" the contact with the officer. Therefore, the contact is not a seizure. The "free to decline" test has been applied by the United States Supreme Court in several cases, including *United States v. Drayton*, 536 U.S. 194 (2002), *Florida v. Bostick*, 501 U.S. 429 (1991), and *INS v. Delgado*, 466 U.S. 210 (1984).

More frequently, however, the "free to leave" test will be sufficient to govern the categorization of the contact. Example: An officer observes a young man walking in an area where a number of burglaries have occurred recently. With no other specific information in mind, the officer approaches the citizen and says, "Excuse me sir, may I speak with you for a moment?" The man stops and says, "Yeah, what is it?" The officer identifies himself and asks if he could see some identification, which the man agreeably produces. The officer asks a few questions, and the two part ways. Because the officer said and did nothing that would cause a reasonable person to feel restrained or otherwise required to participate in the contact, this contact is entirely voluntary in the legal sense.

The Supreme Court has held that, if all a police officer does is approach a subject, identify himself or herself as a police officer, and ask, in a manner that suggests an option, to speak to the subject, a reasonable person does not feel restrained or required to participate in the transaction. See, for examples, the *Drayton*, *Bostick*, and *Delgado* decisions, above, as well as *Florida v. Royer*, 460 U.S. 491 (1983). Of course, tone of voice and/or other conduct could change the result if used coercively. In *Delgado*, the Supreme Court held that law enforcement officers did not seize members of a factory workforce even though officers were stationed near exits while others approached and questioned the workers inside. See also *United States v. Ojeda-Ramos*, 455 F.3d 1178 (10th Cir. 2006), where the Court held that a passenger ordered (along with others) to leave a bus during a scheduled stop was not seized.

The key to creating a voluntary contact is to request cooperation in a manner that suggests an option or simply to strike up a normal, non-coercive conversation.

For an officer, the key to creating a voluntary contact is to request cooperation in a manner that suggests an option or simply to strike up a normal, non-coercive conversation. The officer's exact words are critical. The officer must request or invite the subject's participation, not order, demand, require, instruct, or otherwise coerce it. Evidence of the officer's exact words may include testimony by the officer, the subject, and other witnesses – as well as any recordings that may exist. Non-verbal communication will be relevant as well. While "kind tones" may help, they will not keep plain language from creating a seizure. *See United States v. Richardson,* 385 F.3d 625 (6th Cir. 2004).

What Is The Effect Of Miranda Warnings On Whether A Contact Is Voluntary?

***Miranda* warnings may be counter-purposeful for the officer trying to achieve, and prove, a non-custodial (non-seizure) environment.**

Miranda warnings may be counter-purposeful for the officer trying to achieve, and prove, a non-custodial (non-seizure) environment. Given that federal law requires *Miranda* warnings only in custodial interrogations, a reasonable person who is advised of *Miranda* rights might reasonably conclude that he is in custody, i.e. that he has been seized. To avoid this problem, some officers, instead of explaining custodial interrogation rights (*Miranda* rights) in a non-custodial setting, spend the same time explaining and assuring that the contact is in fact non-custodial. Example: "Billy, you are not under arrest and you're free to leave at anytime. We're just asking for your voluntary cooperation. Would you be willing to discuss this matter with us?"

When circumstances would cause a reasonable person to feel that he is being subjected to restraints normally associated with an arrest, interrogative questions by police require prior warning and waiver of *Miranda* rights. Interrogation of a suspect without *Miranda* warning and waiver is permitted as long as officers have not said or done anything that would cause a reasonable person to feel that he is under arrest at the time of the questioning. *Berkemer v. McCarty*, 468 U.S. 420 (1984); *Stansbury v. California*, 511 U.S. 318 (1994). [NOTE: The law of interrogation, including *Miranda* principles, is covered more thoroughly starting at page 68.]

Investigative Stops And Arrests

If an officer-citizen contact is a seizure within the meaning of the Fourth Amendment, it next must be determined what kind of seizure has occurred.

If an officer-citizen contact is a seizure within the meaning of the Fourth Amendment, it next must be determined what kind of seizure has occurred. There are two possibilities: arrest and investigative detention, or "stop." In this discussion, the terms "investigative detention," "detention," and "stop" are used interchangeably and have identical meanings. Such actions are also often called "*Terry* Stops", referring to *Terry v. Ohio*, 392 U.S. 1 (1968), the Supreme Court's landmark stop and frisk case.

Because investigative detentions and arrests are seizures, they implicate the Fourth Amendment and its "reasonableness" requirements. This means showing certain pre-existing levels of factual justification – reasonable suspicion for stops, probable cause for arrests. But how does one determine whether a seizure is a stop or an arrest?

Is The Seizure An Investigative Stop Or An Arrest?

Deciding whether a seizure is an investigative stop or an arrest requires a determination of "whether...arrest-like measures implemented can nevertheless be reconciled with the limited nature of a *Terry*-type stop." *United States v. Acosta-Colon*, 157 F.3d 9 (1st Cir. 1998). Courts tend to isolate three issues in order to determine whether a seizure is "arrest-like" or "*Terry*-type": (1) The duration of the seizure; (2) whether the seized individual has been involuntarily moved from one place to another; and (3) whether physical force and/or restraints were used. Naturally, the words "you're under arrest" also would be determinative.

How The Duration Of The Seizure Affects Whether The Seizure Is An Investigative Stop Or An Arrest.

Investigative detentions must be brief.

Investigative detentions must be brief. Normally, issues involved in an investigative detention may be resolved in minutes (not hours) and should therefore be completed in that time. In some cases, particularly serious ones where investigation is progressing efficiently toward a determination of presence or absence of probable cause, a detention of an hour or more may be reasonable and therefore constitutional. *See United States v. Gil*, 204 F.3d 1347 (11th Cir. 2000) (75 minutes) and *United States v. McCarthy*, 77 F.3d 522 (1st Cir. 1996) (also 75 minutes) as examples. Stops of much more than an hour are likely to be recategorized as arrests and would therefore require probable cause for their justification. For example, *see United States v. Codd*, 956 F.2d 1109 (11th Cir. 1992), where the Court found that a two-and-a-half-hour detention "went far beyond the boundaries of *Terry*."

In *United States v. Sharpe*, 470 U.S. 675 (1985), the Supreme Court dealt with a case where law enforcement officers performing surveillance in an unmarked car developed reasonable suspicion that a particular pickup truck was illegally transporting drugs. A sedan was traveling in tandem with the truck. After following the vehicles for a number of miles, the officers decided to conduct an investigative stop and radioed another officer for assistance. When the officers attempted to stop the two vehicles, the sedan stopped but the truck continued with the newly-joined assisting officer following. The originally-involved officers talked with the sedan driver and, after first obtaining his driver's license, left the sedan and its driver with a fourth officer and begin looking for the truck and the assisting officer. They found that the assisting officer had stopped the truck and detained its driver. Twenty minutes after the truck was stopped, the initiating officers arrived, put their noses against the rear window of the truck and smelled marijuana. The issue: Was the detection of the marijuana odor part of a lawful investigative detention or had the stop at that point exceeded permissible time limits? The Court held that the truck transaction was a proper investigative detention. There was reasonable suspicion and the roughly 20-minute detention was reasonable. The detection of the odor of marijuana and consequent development of probable cause to search occurred during a period of lawful investigative detention. The probable cause to search justified the opening of the camper shell; the then-found drug evidence was therefore obtained lawfully.

In *United States v. Place*, 462 U.S. 696 (1983), another Supreme Court decision involving time limits of investigative detention, two officers on duty at a major airport approached a subject reasonably suspected of drug courier activity and requested permission to search his luggage. Though the suspect consented to the search, it was not conducted because the suspect's flight was about to leave. The officers called drug interdiction agents at the destination airport and informed them of the reasonable suspicion. Agents at the destination airport approached the suspect after he claimed his luggage. When the suspect refused to consent to a search of the bag, officers told him they were going to take his luggage and attempt to obtain a search warrant, and that he could accompany them if he desired. The suspect declined.

They then took his luggage to another nearby airport where a trained narcotics detection dog was available to conduct a sniff test, which was positive for drugs. Approximately 90 minutes had elapsed between the time the bag was detained and the time of the sniff test. The subject was subsequently arrested for possession of cocaine. The issue: Did the detention of the luggage (based on reasonable suspicion) exceed permissible time limits before the sniff test was performed and probable cause was established?

The Supreme Court concluded that the seizure of the bag exceeded permissible time limits for an investigative detention. The Court noted that the agents knew the suspect would be arriving at the destination airport and they could have and should have arranged for the dog to be at that location. By showing such concern over the 90-minute detention of a piece of luggage (with reasonable suspicion but not probable cause), the Court gave clear indication that the investigative detention of persons for such a period would be closely scrutinized and that investigative detentions must be limited to periods of diligent, active investigation. In less serious matters, even an hour could be too long for an investigative stop supported by less than probable cause. If initial investigation reveals the need for other or different investigation, the duration of the stop may sometimes be extended slightly. See, for example, *United States v. Soto-Cervantes*, 138 F.3d 1319 (10th Cir. 1998) (one-hour stop permitted).

In less serious matters, even an hour could be too long for an investigative stop supported by less than probable cause.

How The Involuntary Movement Of The Detainee Affects Whether A Seizure Is An Investigative Stop Or An Arrest

In *Florida v. Royer*, 460 U.S. 491 (1983), the Supreme Court (in a plurality opinion) ruled that the involuntary movement of a detained subject from an airport concourse to a small, police-controlled room 40 feet away, for purposes of facilitating a luggage search, created an arrest-like transaction that therefore required pre-existing probable cause. However, the Court went on to explain:

"There are undoubtedly reasons of safety and security that would justify moving a suspect from one location to another during an investigatory detention, such as from an airport concourse to a more private area."

Movement of a detainee even a short distance, in the absence of legitimate and articulated safety and security justifications, may create an arrest requiring probable cause.

Thus, movement of a detainee even a short distance, in the absence of legitimate and articulated safety and security justifications, may create an arrest requiring probable cause though the encounter only lasts a few minutes. For an example of the safety and security exception at work *see United States v. $109,179 in U.S. Currency*, 228 F.3d 1080 (9th Cir. 2000)(subject was moved from one motel room to another without creating an arrest at that point). Just saying the words "safety and security" may not suffice as the required articulation – the factual basis for the safety or security concern must be stated. *United States v. Acosta-Colon*, 157 F.3d 9 (1st Cir. 1998).

In the *Royer* case, above, officers approached a subject in an airport concourse because particular aspects of his conduct and demeanor were consistent with a drug courier profile. The officers identified themselves and asked if the subject had a moment to talk. He responded affirmatively. Officers then asked to see his airline ticket and some other form of identification, which he produced. His airline ticket was in the name "Holt" and his driver's license in the name "Royer." Asked to explain the two names, he became very nervous and failed to give a reasonable explanation. Officers then informed the subject that he was suspected of drug smuggling and, without returning his driver's license or ticket, asked him to accompany them to a room approximately 40 feet away. There, officers obtained consent to search his luggage. Drugs were found during the consent search. Issue: Was the consent search the product of a lawful investigative detention or an unlawful arrest?

As mentioned above, the Court, in a plurality opinion, held that the evidence from the consent search was the product of a police action that was either an arrest or so arrest-like as to require pre-existing probable cause. Because there was not yet probable cause to arrest at the time the involuntary movement was undertaken, the resulting evidence was inadmissible. However, also as mentioned above, the Court noted that the result could have been different if the officers had explained in their testimony legitimate safety or security reasons for the short movement.

Two years later, in *Hayes v. Florida*, 470 U.S. 811 (1985), the Court dealt similarly with the issue of the involuntary movement of a suspect. Officers conducting a felony investigation had a principal suspect but insufficient evidence to arrest him. When latent prints were found in the victim's bedroom, officers decided to visit the suspect's home to obtain his fingerprints. They did not seek a court order authorizing this procedure. The suspect spoke with officers on the front porch of his home and told them he did not want to go to the police station for fingerprinting. An officer responded, "Sir, if you don't come with me, I will have to place you under arrest." The suspect replied, "In that case I will go." He was then taken to the police station and fingerprinted. Issue: Was the resulting fingerprint evidence the product of a lawful investigative detention or an unlawful (arrest-type) transaction?

The Court held that the transaction was, in essence, an illegal arrest. The officer's method of getting the suspect to accompany him to the station was a seizure, because a reasonable person would have felt that he was required to go with the officer. Because the seizure involved involuntary movement from place to place, it was sufficiently like an arrest as to require probable cause to arrest at that point. Evidence resulting from the seizure was product of an illegality - fruit of a poisoned tree.

Earlier, in *Dunaway v. New York*, 442 U.S. 200 (1979), the Supreme Court had reached a like decision on similar facts. In *Kaupp v. Texas*, 538 U.S. 626 (2003), the Court restated its view that involuntary movement of a seized person to another place is, in essence, an arrest. Importantly, *Dunaway*, *Hayes* and *Kaupp* all involved requiring a person to accompany police to a law enforcement facility. Only *Royer* involved movement to some other place. Lower courts are split (as was the *Royer* court) on whether requiring a detained person to move to a non-police dominated location would be an arrest (for example, moving someone from one public location to another public location). Some courts have held that moving a detained person to another nearby location for a show-up (one-on-one) identification is not

Lower courts are split on whether requiring a detained person to move to a non-police dominated location would be an arrest.

an arrest. See, as examples, *United States v. McCargo*, 464 F.3d 192 (2d Cir. 2006) and *United States v. Martinez*, 462 F.3d 903 (8th Cir. 2006). Because of confusion in this area of the law, the better course may be for officers to have the eyewitness come to the place of the detention, rather than require the detainee to go to the location of the eyewitness.

How The Use Of Force And/Or Restraints Affects Whether A Seizure Is An Investigatory Stop Or An Arrest

Non-deadly force and other restraints may be used as reasonably necessary to effect and safely maintain an investigative detention; such actions do not automatically convert the transaction into an arrest. In fact, in the original "stop and frisk" case, the Supreme Court approved the seizure of a person on less than probable cause where a police officer "grabbed [a subject] and spun him around" before proceeding with a frisk. *Terry v. Ohio*, 88 392 U.S. 1 (1968).

In a variety of lower court decisions, the use of reasonable force in investigative stops has been approved up to and including stops conducted at gunpoint. Thus, even the show of deadly force does not necessarily convert a detention into an arrest, as long as there is strong justification for the force or show of force. See, as examples, *United States v. Heath*, 259 F.3d 522 (6th Cir. 2001) and *United States v. Rousseau*, 257 F.3d 925 (9th Cir. 2001). Similarly, blocking an escape path, handcuffing and/or locking the suspect in a police vehicle may be appropriate in some investigative detentions where reasonably necessary to ensure officer safety or security of the detainee. *See United States v. Felix-Felix*, 275 F.3d 627 (7th Cir. 2001) and *United States v. Yang*, 286 F.3d 940 (7th Cir. 2002).

Handcuffing and/or locking the suspect in a police vehicle may be appropriate in some investigative detentions where reasonably necessary to ensure officer safety or security of the detainee.

Thus, an officer may use force as reasonably necessary – including touching, grabbing, or pointing a gun – in order to stop a person. However, if there is more force than reasonably necessary, a court may determine that the seizure was an arrest and therefore required pre-existing probable cause. *See Park v. Shiflett*, 250 F.3d 843 (4th Cir. 2001) as an example.

When "Unarrest" Is Necessary

Perhaps the strange word "unarrest" should be replaced with a phrase that sounds more "legal": "Discontinuation of arrest custody upon dissipation and/or evaporation of probable cause." In any event, it is the view of many police law experts that if, after making an arrest, an officer discovers that probable cause did not exist in the first place or has now evaporated, the subject should be released as quickly as possible. This would occur, ideally, in a safe place, preferably of the arrestee's choosing. It is not necessary or desirable that the arrestee be further processed or presented to a judicial official. Instead, the details of the arrest and unarrest should be thoroughly documented, along with the justifications for each. A compelling argument exists that continued custody after the evaporation of probable cause for an arrest violates the Fourth Amendment. On such facts, "unarrest" may be constitutionally imperative. See, as examples, *McConney v. City of Houston*, 863 F.2d 1180 (5th Cir. 1989); *BeVier v. Hucal*, 806 F.2d 123 (7th Cir. 1986)(dicta); and *Thompson v. Olson*, 798 F.2d 552 (1st Cir. 1986)(dicta). This may be true notwithstanding state statutory law requiring that "upon making an arrest, the officer shall present the arrestee to a judicial officer without unnecessary delay." Such statutes exist to assure proper handling of people who are being kept in custody, not those being released from it.

In some circumstances, "unarrest" may be constitutionally imperative.

"Seizures" And The *Miranda* Rule

Although the *Miranda* rule is discussed in more depth later, it should be noted here that one consequence of the categorization of an officer-citizen contact is its effect on whether or not *Miranda* warning and waiver procedures are required prior to questioning of the subject. Ironically, the simplest part of the *Miranda* rule is the most frequently misunderstood. The rule applies only when a person is interrogated while in police "custody." *Miranda v. Arizona*, 384 U.S. 436 (1966). The test for *Miranda* "custody" is objective: Would a reasonable person feel that he was subjected to restraints normally associated with for-

Ironically, the simplest part of the Miranda rule is the most frequently misunderstood.

mal arrest? The subjective feelings of a particular subject are of no consequence in deciding whether the subject is in custody for *Miranda* purposes. The question is: Has the officer said and/or done things that a reasonable person normally associates with being arrested? *Berkemer v. McCarty*, 468 U.S. 420 (1984).

When a subject comes to and remains at the interrogation site on a voluntary basis there is no *Miranda* custody, even when suspicion is "focused" and there is accusatory interrogation. *Oregon v. Mathiason*, 429 U.S. 492 (1977). A roadside stop (investigative detention) is not "custody" for purposes of *Miranda*, but an arrest is. *Berkemer v. McCarty*, 468 U.S. 420 (1984). Custody, not focus of suspicion, determines whether a person to be interrogated is entitled to *Miranda* warnings. *Beckwith v. United States*, 425 U.S. 341 (1976). The concept of "custody" for purposes of *Miranda* is almost identical to the Fourth Amendment concept of "arrest" but is slightly broader. It includes those investigative detentions that are so arrest-like that reasonable people could mistake them for an arrest. Gun pointing, handcuffing, and locking someone in the back of a police car may all be reasonable parts of some *Terry* stops but those measures could easily be viewed by a reasonable person as the beginning of an arrest. Consequently, they may also signal the beginning of *Miranda* custody.

CHAPTER 3

REASONABLE SUSPICION AND PROBABLE CAUSE

Unless and until facts and circumstances combine in certain legally sufficient ways, a police officer has no authority to infringe upon anyone's freedom or reasonable privacy expectations.

The Fourth Amendment to the United States Constitution requires that all searches and seizures be "reasonable." Such police actions are "reasonable" only if there are facts and circumstances that justify them. Unless and until facts and circumstances combine in certain legally sufficient ways, a police officer has no authority to infringe upon anyone's freedom or reasonable privacy expectations.

The factual combinations that justify various searches and seizures have been given names in the law. Some police actions - arrests and full searches, for example - require an amount of factual justification called "probable cause." Certain limited police actions - investigative stops and weapons frisks, as examples - do not require as much factual justification. They are justified by combinations called "reasonable suspicion."

Reasonable suspicion and probable cause are fluid and shifting concepts that depend on the specific facts and circumstances of a situation. Each case is unique. Probable cause and/or reasonable suspicion will crystallize only on the basis of the particular facts of a particular case.

The Definition Of Probable Cause And Reasonable Suspicion

Terminology is important. The terms "reasonable suspicion" and "probable cause" should be used carefully and precisely. The term "probable cause" often is used loosely and mistakenly to describe any lawful basis for an investigative action. That is, when a prosecutor or a judge says that an officer lacked probable cause to stop a vehicle, that person often really means the officer did not "have authority" to stop the vehicle. This loose usage of the term "probable cause" creates confusion and generates problems in criminal prosecutions. An officer can "have authority" to stop a vehicle even when he does not have "probable cause." Many searches and seizures may be justified by a factual basis significantly less than probable cause. Reasonable suspicion will justify many police actions and is much easier to establish. See, for example, *United States v. Sokolow*, 490 U.S. 1 (1981). The distinctions between probable cause and reasonable suspicion are significant.

Here are some working definitions:

Probable Cause: Facts and circumstances which, taken together with rational inferences therefrom, would cause a reasonable police officer to **believe**...

a. (To arrest)...that a crime has been committed and that a particular person committed it;

b. (To search)...that evidence of a crime is in the place to be searched;

c. (To seize)...that items are contraband or otherwise evidence of crime, or are lawfully subject to forfeiture to the government under applicable forfeiture laws.

Reasonable Suspicion: Facts and circumstances which, taken together with rational inferences therefore, would cause a reasonable police officer to **suspect**...

a. (To detain or "stop")...that a person is, has been, or is about to be, involved in criminal activity;

b. (To frisk a person)...that a person subject to lawful detention is armed and constitutes a danger to the officer;

c. (To frisk other areas)...that an area within the immediate control and access of a person lawfully detained contains weapons and that the detainee might use those weapons against the officer;

d. (To conduct a "protective sweep")...that other rooms or spaces in a place where an officer is lawfully present contains would-be assailants who would constitute a threat to the officer.

Establishing Probable Cause And Reasonable Suspicion

Establishing probable cause and reasonable suspicion requires that facts, circumstances, and inferences be articulable – explainable in words.

Establishing probable cause and reasonable suspicion requires that facts, circumstances, and inferences be articulable – explainable in words. Neither probable cause nor reasonable suspicion may be based solely on an unexplainable "hunch" or feeling. In fact, reasonable suspicion is sometimes referred to as "articulable suspicion." In developing inferences, a police officer's training and experience may be, and should be, taken into account.

Well-trained and/or experienced officers can detect criminal suspiciousness from circumstances which might be meaningless to untrained and/or inexperienced observers. See, for example, *United States v. Cortez*, 449 U.S. 411 (1981).

Probable cause and reasonable suspicion may be transferred or "imputed." The officer taking an investigative action need not have all operative facts and circumstances in his mind as long as that information is in the mind(s) of others in the chain of investigative action. In fact, if an officer arrests someone on one matter without probable cause, but it turns out that there was probable cause to arrest the person on another matter – of which the arresting officer was originally unaware – the arrest is lawful. *Devenpeck v. Alford*, 543 U.S. 146 (2004). The same appears to be true in the case of stops. See, for example, *United States v. Delfin-Colima*, 464 F.3d 392 (3d Cir. 2006).

Conceptualizing Reasonable Suspicion And Probable Cause

The concepts of probable cause and reasonable suspicion may be viewed as part of a spectrum which could be called a "factual justification continuum." The spectrum might range from "0" (zero) – knowing nothing about a situation – to 100%, being sure or certain of something. It is helpful to look at various factual justifications as they might fall on such a scale.

Absolute certainty is never required in our criminal justice system, even to convict a person in court of a crime.

Absolute certainty is never required in our criminal justice system, even to convict a person in court of a crime. To convict and punish a person for a criminal offense requires "proof beyond a reasonable doubt." If one were to attach a "percentage of certainty" to that, perhaps it might be "98% sure" that a particular person committed a crime.

Below that on a spectrum might be a standard of factual justification called "clear and convincing" evidence. This is the amount of factual justification required in many states to subject a person to involuntary mental commitment. That is, before a person may be involuntarily hospitalized for a mental condition, many states require that there be clear and convincing evidence that a person is a danger to himself or others. This standard might fall above a 50% marker, but below "proof beyond a reasonable doubt."

Just above 50%, but below "clear and convincing," is a standard called "preponderance of the evidence" or the "greater weight of the evidence." It is the standard used in most civil and administrative actions. For the plaintiff to prevail in a civil action, he must prove his case by the preponderance of evidence. If one were attaching a numerical percentage to that concept, it might be roughly "51% sure" – literally the "greater weight."

The preponderance or greater weight standard was traditionally taught to law enforcement officers as the meaning of probable cause. The concept of probable cause was equated to the phrase "more likely than not," which was often illustrated as "51%" or "the greater weight." Since *Illinois v. Gates*, 462 U.S. 213 (1983), it has become clear that probable cause does not require a showing that something is mathematically probable, or more likely than not. Rather, the probable cause standard requires showing "a fair probability" measured in light of common sense and with benefit of the officer's training and experience.

It has become clear that probable cause does not require a showing that something is mathematically probable, or more likely than not.

Thus, probable cause may require (at its lowest levels) something near 50%, but not necessarily 51% or higher. Probable cause can exist even when something is slightly less than mathematically "likely." *See Maryland v. Pringle*, 540 U.S. 366 (2003), where the Supreme Court stated that the preponderance of the evidence standard "has no place" in a probable cause determination. *See also United States v. Romero,* 452 F.3d 610 (6th Cir. 2006) and *United States v. Chauncey*, 420 F.3d 864 (8th Cir. 2005), recent cases applying *Pringle.*

Beneath probable cause on the scale is reasonable suspicion, sometimes called "articulable suspicion." Reasonable suspicion is more than unexplainable hunches or feelings, but less than probable cause. Perhaps reasonable suspicion might be shown at "30 - 40% likely" on the scale.

Reasonable suspicion and probable cause do not necessarily require lots of facts. Courts look not only at the number of facts, but the weight of each fact or circumstance, together with inferences and/or deductions that are reasonable in light of the officer's training and experience. Probable cause or reasonable suspicion could come from just one or two facts if they were strong enough. It is not a matter of just counting facts. Instead, it is a matter of looking at all the facts, assessing the importance of each in the totality of circumstances, and making a common sense judgment in light of training and experience. *United States v. Arvizu*, 534 U.S. 266 (2002). Only then does the officer decide whether there is reasonable suspicion or probable cause. There is no precise formula. *Illinois v. Gates*, 462 U.S. 213 (1983).

Sources Of Information

Where and how is information for reasonable suspicion and probable cause gathered? How does one weigh source information for purposes of reaching conclusions? How does one use sources of information to develop reasonable suspicion and probable cause?

Generally speaking, there are two ways one gains information. One is personal observation or knowledge. That is, we know it ourselves, or we see it, smell it, taste it, or hear it ourselves. Firsthand knowledge obviously is normally most useful. See, for example, *United States v. Bishop*, 264 F.3d 919 (9th Cir. 2001). If information does not come from personal observation, then it came from somewhere else. This might be a document or another person, for example. For purposes of this writing, such information will be called "hearsay."

For purposes of establishing probable cause and/or reasonable suspicion, the use of hearsay information is permitted and normal.

Many officers have been led to believe that hearsay cannot be used in a court proceeding. However, for purposes of establishing probable cause and/or reasonable suspicion, the use of hearsay information is permitted and normal. *See Draper v. United States*, 358 U.S. 307 (1959) and *Jones v. United States*, 362 U.S. 257 (1960).

Not all hearsay is useful for probable cause or reasonable suspicion. If a drunk person who suffers from various mental conditions were to approach an officer and tell him that something happened, the officer might not assign the information much weight. To be the basis for probable cause, hearsay must be reasonably reliable.

To establish reasonable suspicion, supporting hearsay information need not be quite so reliable as that required for probable cause. Because reasonable suspicion is a lower standard of evidence than probable cause, it requires less information and demands less in terms of the reliability of the information source. See, for example, *Alabama v. White*, 496 U.S. 325 (1990).

Because reasonable suspicion is a lower standard of evidence than probable cause, it requires less information and demands less in terms of the reliability of the information source.

To assess the reliability of hearsay, one looks mainly at two things:

1. How reliable is the information provider?
2. How does he know the information?

For example, suppose a person reports to police that there is marijuana growing in John Smith's enclosed backyard patio. One first asks whether that information comes from a reliable person, a person who generally should be believed. If the information has come from a reliable person, one still needs to know how the reliable person came by the information. Did he himself see the marijuana growing in that backyard patio or is he reporting something that he has heard from someone else? If a very reliable person tells an officer something, but the reliable person is only passing on what he has heard from an extremely unreliable or unknown source, the information is not necessarily reliable. One must watch for "layers" of hearsay and look for the reliability of information at each level, or layer. When one attempts to establish probable cause, these questions must be asked more precisely and answers will be judged more critically than when trying to develop reasonable suspicion. See, for example, *United States v. Shaw*, 464 F.3d 615 (6th Cir. 2006), where a mother's "barebones" allegation to police that her three-year-old son had told her that he had been molested by a particular person created a duty for police to investigate but did not by itself create probable cause to arrest the accused.

Although they are hearsay, police reports and other official police documents are generally presumed to be reliable because they are usually written by other police officers. However, police documents and reports can and often do include layers of hearsay. Often, reports merely document what someone told another police officer. So, if the report is telling one officer what someone told another police officer, there are two layers of hearsay. If a person telling something to the officer completing the report is merely relating something that the person did not see himself, but heard from someone else, there are three layers of hearsay:

1. The report itself.
2. The person providing information to the reporting officer.
3. The person who provided the original information.

The officer seeking to use the report for purposes of reasonable suspicion and/or probable cause must consider the reliability of the information at each layer. When one presumes that police reports and documents are reliable, one is only presuming that the reporting officer has accurately and truthfully documented what he has been told. That is not necessarily the same thing as believing what he was told.

Source Credibility: Why Should This Source Be Believed?

Police Officers

Reasonable suspicion and probable cause generally may be transferred, or "imputed," from one officer or police workgroup to another.

If Police Officer A tells Officer B that A saw something himself, it is reasonable for B to believe it. In the absence of any reason to disbelieve Officer A, if he says he saw it, heard it, tasted it, smelled it, or felt it himself, it is reasonable to believe that Officer A is telling the truth and that it is an accurate report of a personal observation. This issue is long settled. *United States v. Ventresca*, 380 U.S. 102 (1965). This is why reasonable suspicion and probable cause generally may be transferred, or "imputed," from one officer or police workgroup to another. *See Whitely v. Warden, Wyoming State Penitentiary*, 401 U.S. 560 (1971), *United States v. Fiasconaro*, 315 F.3d 28 (1st Cir. 2002), and *United States v. Sandoval-Venegas*, 292 F.3d 1101 (9th Cir. 2002), as examples.

Concerned Citizens

What about other people – just concerned, regular citizens – who state to police that they saw or heard things? May these people be believed for purposes of establishing reasonable suspicion and probable cause? To answer that question, one asks another. Does the source (the ordinary concerned citizen) have any known reason to lie to the police? If the answer to that question is "no," then courts usually presume the information to be reliable. *See Guzell v. Hiller*, 223 F.3d 518 (7th Cir. 2000).

Again, one must be alert for layers of hearsay. If a concerned citizen source tells police that something occurred, police must ask whether the source was the one who heard, saw, tasted, touched, or smelled it himself – or is he merely reporting what some other person observed? Assuming that the ordinary concerned citizen is reporting a personal observation and has no apparent reason to lie, it is reasonable to believe that the observation is accurate and/or that the statement is likely true. This would be "reasonably reliable" hearsay. *See United States v. Harris*, 403 U.S. 573 (1971) and *Kiser v. City of Huron*, 219 F.3d 814 (8th Cir. 2000).

Criminal Informants

Criminal informants are a different matter. There is reason to suspect or doubt information that is given by people who are known to be involved in criminal activity. Reasonably reliable information can come from criminals, but more must be done to verify the information - to establish reasons to believe it. See, for example, *United States v. Barnes*, 195 F.3d 1027 (8th Cir. 1999).

Several factors may make it reasonable to believe information provided by criminal informants.

Several factors may make it reasonable to believe information provided by criminal informants. Some criminal informants are paid, which provides at least some incentive to tell the truth. Most such informants realize that if they are not truthful and accurate, they are not likely to continue to be paid for their information.

Another factor is whether the informant has some sort of "track record" – a history of being reliable and providing accurate information. See, for example, *United States v. Sidwell*, 440 F.3d 865 (7th Cir. 2006). A history or track record of reliability furnishes a basis for believing that the source is reliable. It helps even more if that information has led to arrests, seizures of evidence, and/or convictions in court.

Another way to establish reliability is to verify details of what the informant says. If he tells police that certain facts (X, Y, Z) are true, and if X and Y can be verified as accurate information, it becomes more reasonable to believe that Z is also likely to be true. That sort of verification, checking to see if information is accurate, is called "corroboration." Corroboration can be important and is sometimes required in establishing reasonable suspicion and probable cause. However, if an informant has a sufficient track record of providing accurate information, little or no corroboration may be necessary. See, e.g. *United States v. Riley*, 351 F.3d 1265 (D.C. Cir. 2003).

Confidential Informants

Some informants are willing to have their names used in connection with their information and some are not. This is true for both criminal informants and concerned citizen informants. The primary reason that people, ordinary concerned citizens and criminals alike, are unwilling to have their names used is that they fear repercussions and/or retaliation. In some cases, they fear for their safety and their lives. Because police know who the source is, it is often permissible to use such information to establish reasonable suspicion and probable cause even though the source is unwilling to have his name disclosed.

If the informant is also a witness to the crime being prosecuted, it may be necessary for the prosecution to either identify the witness or dismiss the case.

In such a case, however, it is critical to document (and explain in court, if necessary) why the source does not wish to be named. It may also be necessary to provide information confirming that the informant, though unnamed, does in fact exist. If the informant is also a witness to the crime being prosecuted, it may be necessary for the prosecution to either identify the witness or dismiss the case. *See Roviaro v. United States*, 353 U.S. 53 (1957).

Anonymous Tips

Because it is unlikely that an anonymous source will have a known track record of reliability, in order to form probable cause from an anonymous tip one would need significant corroboration of certain types of information. Some facts would have to be verified in order to believe that other facts provided were likely to be true. So, an anonymous tip can provide the starting point, but the amount and type of tip information that can be corroborated will determine whether the tip ultimately leads to reasonable suspicion or probable cause. Anonymous tips that accurately predict future behavior seem to have the best chance of measuring up to legal standards. See, for example, *Alabama v. White*, 496 U.S. 325 (1990) (anonymous tip plus corroboration enough for reasonable suspicion) and *Illinois v. Gates*, 462 U.S. 213 (1983) (anonymous tip plus corroboration good for probable cause.) But in *Florida v. J. L.*, 529 U.S. 266 (2000), the Supreme Court held that an anonymous tip that a described person at a described public place was carrying a gun is not, without more, sufficient for reasonable suspicion to stop and frisk, even though corroboration of description, time and place occurred. In *Draper v. United States*, 358 U.S. 307 (1959) and *Illinois v. Gates*, 462 U.S. 213 (1983), the Supreme Court found that probable cause could be developed through an officer's corroboration of certain neutral details of an anonymous tip regarding criminal activity. Since that is enough, in some circumstances, to establish probable cause, then obviously reasonable suspicion sometimes may be established by a partially-corroborated anonymous tip. *See Alabama v. White*, 496 U.S. 325 (1990), *but compare Florida v. J. L.*, 529 U.S. 266 (2000) for a contrary result in light of differing facts. In *United States v. Long*, 464 F.3d 569 (6th Cir. 2006), a federal appeals court held that a caller who tells police that he is the neighbor of a home then being burglarized is a presumptively reliable citizen informant, not an anonymous source, even though his name was not obtained.

An anonymous tip can provide the starting point, but the amount and type of tip information that can be corroborated will determine whether the tip ultimately leads to reasonable suspicion or probable cause.

Frequently Recurring Factors

Geographical Location Of The Subject

In developing probable cause and/or reasonable suspicion, it is appropriate to consider a person's location. Suppose a person is walking down a sidewalk at night. Walking on a sidewalk is not itself unusual or suspicious. There is no reason to suspect the person of criminal activity based on his location. But suppose a person is hidden in the bushes behind a warehouse. In the latter situation, the subject's location is appropriately a suspicion factor. If a subject's geographical location is very close to the scene of a recently-committed crime then typically the location factor grows in its significance.

High Crime Area

Suppose the subject is in a neighborhood or an area of town which has been experiencing a very high crime rate. Suppose the subject is on a particular street corner that is very well known for hand-to-hand sales of drugs. In such cases, the subject's location would become a suspicion factor. See, for example, *United States v. Lindsey*, 482 F.3d 1285 (11th Cir. 2007) (corroborated anonymous tip plus presence in a high crime area).

If a person is walking down the sidewalk at 3 a.m. in an otherwise deserted neighborhood in which there has recently been a rash of nighttime crime, those factors could all be considered in measuring for reasonable suspicion. Officers may take into account all the factors present and judge them in their totality, all things considered. *United States v. Arvizu*, 534 U.S. 266 (2002).

A Caution On The "High Crime Area" Factor

The fact that there have been crimes in the past in a given area does not make that area forever thereafter a high crime area.

The fact that there have been crimes in the past in a given area does not make that area forever thereafter a high crime area. For an area to be labeled a "high crime area," that label needs to be true in an objective sense – in a way that can be articulated and justified – that there has been some sort of spree or real history of continued crime in this particular area. Statistical comparison to other areas might make the high crime area label more appropriate and significant. It is important that officers not fall into the habit of describing all parts of the community as high crime areas just because there has been some crime in those areas historically.

Time Factor

When is a subject observed? If he is observed very near the place of a crime very soon after a crime has been committed, those two factors combine to assume greater importance. The longer after the crime a person is observed the less significant the location factor becomes.

Presence of a person in public, even late at night, is not enough by itself to justify an investigative detention or arrest.

Presence of a person in public, even late at night, is not enough by itself to justify an investigative detention or arrest. With the possible exception of curfews, there is no hour of the night so late that people are generally subject to seizure just for being in public. If a person is walking down a sidewalk at 4:00 a.m., that by itself does not justify an investigative detention. Of course, an officer may approach such a person and attempt to engage him in voluntary contact and conversation. The officer must take care, however, not to allow the contact to escalate into a seizure unless reasonable suspicion or probable cause has developed.

Sensory Perceptions

An officer's sense of smell may be extremely important.

Obviously, seeing something suspicious should cause suspicion. Hearing suspicious noises should do likewise. An officer's sense of smell may be extremely important. If, with benefit of training and/or experience, an officer is able to recognize certain odors as suggesting the presence and/or use of illegal drugs, that sensory perception by itself may establish reasonable suspicion or probable cause. See, for example, *United States v. Humphries*, 372 F.3d 653 (4th Cir. 2004). Similarly, if during a lawful weapons frisk an officer should touch or feel objects that, though hidden from view, are recognizably a form of contraband (like illegal drugs), the sensory perception may be used for or toward conclusions of reasonable suspicion or probable cause. *See Minnesota v. Dickerson*, 508 U.S. 366 (1993).

Suspect And Criminal Description Similarities

Obviously, if a person closely resembles the description of a person who has committed a crime, there may be reason to believe or suspect that the person might have been the one who committed the crime. How close a fit must there be between the subject's appearance and the reported description? Certainly, a tighter fit is required in order to establish probable cause. A looser or more general similarity can sometimes be sufficient to establish reasonable suspicion.

Just one aspect of a physical description could be enough to justify a seizure of a person if the descriptors were sufficiently rare. If the only thing known about the person who committed a crime ten minutes ago is that he was wearing pink high top tennis shoes with purple stars drawn on them, that in itself would likely provide lawful basis for a seizure of a person who fit this one factor description, because the factor is so particular and so unusual.

But what if the perpetrator of a summertime, midmorning crime was reported to have been a white male in his mid-twenties wearing blue jeans and a T-shirt? If an officer were to see, a half-mile from the crime scene, an hour after the reported crime, in a densely populated urban setting, a person who fit that description, the description match might be of little significance. However, that same description, at a different time of day, a different location relative to a crime scene, and in an area of lesser population density, might provide the basis for probable cause or reasonable suspicion.

The Suspect's Observed Behaviors

Another important factor is the suspect's behavior before he knows police are present. Is the subject observed, for example, carrying a bag of tools to the back of a warehouse? Is he carrying a gas can to the back of a closed and inactive business late at night? Extreme nervousness and "furtive" gestures also may be considered.

Also significant is a subject's behavior after he sees or is contacted by the police. Again, extreme and unusual nervousness may be considered. Attempts to evade contact with police and certainly out-and-out flight – running in apparent panic at the sight of police – may be considered strong suspicion factors. If an officer were to drive behind a closed and inactive warehouse at two o'clock in the morning and a man standing behind the warehouse were to run when he saw the officer, these facts and circumstances taken together almost certainly form reasonable suspicion that this person is involved in criminal activity.

While running at the sight of police is suspicious, it is not likely, by itself, to establish reasonable suspicion. In *California v. Hodari D.*, 499 U.S. 621 (1991), the Supreme Court approached this issue but did not settle it. It is best to assume that at least one additional suspicion factor is required to establish reasonable suspicion, especially in light of *Illinois v. Wardlow*, 528 U.S. 119 (2000), where it took a 5 – 4 decision of the Supreme Court to find that running at the sight of police, plus presence in an area well known for illegal drug activity, were together enough for reasonable suspicion. *See also United States v. Mayo*, 361 F.3d 802 (4th Cir. 2004), for a more recent application of this principle. A passenger "bolting" from a car stopped for a traffic violation creates reasonable suspicion, according to a federal appeals court in *United States v. Bonner*, 263 F.3d 213 (3d Cir. 2004).

While running at the sight of police is suspicious, it is not likely, by itself, to establish reasonable suspicion.

Knowledge Of A Subject's Criminal History Or Past Criminal Behavior

What if an officer sees someone walking down the street late at night that the officer knows has a lengthy criminal record of house-breaking and store-breaking offenses? While knowledge of the subject's history and/or criminal record may be taken into account as a suspicion factor, it usually cannot be the exclusive basis for a stop. A person who in the past has been convicted of crime does not lose forever his right to walk freely in public. He may not be stopped solely because he has a record.

A person who in the past has been convicted of crime does not lose forever his right to walk freely in public.

But suppose an officer is patrolling a part of town where there has been a recent crime spree involving late-night break-ins. Suppose as well that it is late at night and the officer sees a person the officer knows has a lengthy history of break-in and related offenses. In those circumstances, the subject's record could be strongly considered in the development of reasonable suspicion or probable cause.

Profiling

As an officer gains training and experience, it becomes possible to form reasonable inferences from certain characteristics and behavioral patterns which the trained, experienced officer recognizes as consistent with statistical "profiles" of certain types of criminals and/or criminal behavior. In particular, profiling is often successful in drug enforcement, where some officers possess an enormous backlog of experience and insight which, through training, may be extended to other officers. The Supreme Court held in *United States v. Sokolow*, 490 U.S.1 (1989), that it is possible to form reasonable suspicion from factors all of which come from a profile, and from behaviors which, taken individually, are entirely innocent.

It is possible to form reasonable suspicion from factors all of which come from a profile, and from behaviors which, taken individually, are entirely innocent.

It is critical that officers evaluate profile matches in light of all surrounding circumstances and common sense. Profiling should not be done rigidly or mechanically as if it were a simple checklist. The use of race as a factor in profiling is generally inappropriate and usually illegal. Officers must stay closely apprised of both law and policy in this turbulent area but "profiling," absent illegal discrimination, is not unconstitutional.

Unusualness

In the past, some case law and a considerable amount of police training suggested that it is "suspicious" if someone is "out of place" or "unusual" in a particular area or neighborhood, particularly during nighttime hours. The conclusion that someone "doesn't belong in" a certain neighborhood also feeds this notion of "suspiciousness." Obviously, one way someone could be judged "unusual" or "out of place" is that his race is inconsistent with neighborhood demographics. Because such judgments, whether reached by "concerned citizens" or by officers, create much potential for racially discriminatory police actions, it is probably wise for police to discount this factor, however "common-sensical" some might feel it to be.

The fact that something or someone is unusual in a particular setting is not necessarily criminally suspicious.

The fact that something or someone is unusual in a particular setting is not necessarily criminally suspicious. People wearing top hats and riding unicycles are unusual but presumably not thereby criminally suspicious. In the desert, both rain and rainbows are unusual – but neither are criminally suspicious. For the "unusual" consequently to be judged suspicious, two more dots must be connected. The particular "unusualness" must also suggest criminal involvement. While some forms of unusualness will satisfy this criterion, a person's skin pigmentation, regardless of neighborhood or hour of the day or night, will not.

Uncooperativeness

What about a person who is very uncooperative when confronted by police? Suppose, for example, that an officer (without reasonable suspicion) walks up to a person and attempts a voluntary contact. The officer says, "Excuse me, sir, do you have a moment I could speak with you?" The subject responds, "No way, I'm in a big hurry. I've got to go."

Suppose the police officer walks along with him (which is permitted) and says, "Sir, where are you going in such a hurry?" Suppose further that the person now gets verbally abusive toward the officer, questioning the officer's motives, saying, "Look, Butthead, why are you harassing me?" The Officer replies, "Sir, do you mind if I see some identification?" The man refuses to produce identification, saying, "I'm not showing you any identification. I told you I was in a hurry," and turns to walk away.

In such a situation, lack of cooperation cannot serve as the foundation for reasonable suspicion or probable cause. In general people are normally under no legal obligation to cooperate with police, to answer any questions, or to provide any documentation of their identities.

Even if there is reason to suspect a person of criminal activity and that person is detained (stopped), that person generally possesses a constitutionally-guarded right of privacy in respect to the contents of his or her pockets, wallet, or purse. The refusal to relinquish a constitutionally-protected right cannot be used by police as justification for the seizure of a person or for a police-ordered inspection of personal documents. Similarly, a person generally cannot be stopped or arrested for his failure to "explain himself" (i.e., to "justify" his presence in a given place) or even verbal abuse (including profanity and vulgarity) toward the officer. *See Johnson v. Campbell*, 332 F.3d 199 (3d Cir. 2003).

The refusal to relinquish a constitutionally-protected right cannot be used by police as justification for the seizure of a person or for a police-ordered inspection of personal documents.

However, a state or local law that requires, in the context of a lawful investigative detention, that a subject verbally identify himself upon demand of police may be constitutional. *Hiibel v. District Court of Nevada*, 542 U.S. 177 (2004). Also, if a person is engaged in activities requiring a privilege license (driving, hunting, fishing as examples) an officer may require production of a privilege license, assuming the officer is not inappropriately singling people out for such contacts. See, for example, *Delaware v. Prouse*, 440 U.S. 648 (1979).

Officers' Collective Knowledge

Who must have reasonable suspicion or probable cause? Can this be a group activity or must reasonable suspicion or probable cause ultimately be consolidated within the mind of an individual officer? The Supreme Court has not addressed the issue and lower courts are fragmented. Some state appeals courts have held that factual justification must exist, at least based on collective knowledge, within the work group of the officer ultimately taking action. In such an analysis, reasonable suspicion or probable cause could exist even though it has not crystallized in the thoughts of any one officer and even though no one particular officer has the whole fact situation in mind. Other courts have required that the factual justification for an action must have congealed in the mind of at least one officer in the chain of action.

The acting officer does not have to learn all the facts and circumstances which are known to the originating (requesting) officer.

If, however, one officer does have reasonable suspicion or probable cause and he asks or orders another officer to make a stop or arrest, the officer taking the action is factually justified based on the theory of transferred or "imputed" justification. The acting officer does not have to learn all the facts and circumstances which are known to the originating (requesting) officer. If the officer initiating the request or order to arrest has reasonable suspicion or probable cause and another officer acts on that officer's request, the second officer is deemed to have acted with benefit of the first officer's knowledge.

Obviously, for there to be the necessary trust relationship between the officer requesting or demanding and the officer who is taking the action requested or demanded, there must be a basis for that trust. This requires that officers making such requests or demands be certain that the required level of factual justification exists before making the request or demand of other officers. *See United States v. Colon*, 250 F.3d 130 (2d Cir. 2001) for an unsuccessful attempt to impute probable cause from a 911 operator to a police officer.

CHAPTER 4

VEHICLE STOPS AND SEARCHES

Though the Supreme Court has explained this area of the law in more than two dozen cases, considerable confusion still exists in lower courts concerning when a vehicle may be stopped, when it may be searched without a warrant, and exactly what portion of the vehicle may be searched. Following is a discussion of vehicle stops, the various types of warrantless vehicle searches, the justification required to conduct each search, and the scope of lawful search, including whether a closed container may be searched. In this discussion, the term "closed container" refers to any container, open or shut, the contents of which are concealed from view and are not readily apparent.

Stopping A Vehicle

With narrow exceptions such as certain types of checkpoints, the same factual justification necessary to validate an investigative detention of a pedestrian is required for the stop of a vehicle to detain an occupant.

With narrow exceptions such as certain types of checkpoints, the same factual justification necessary to validate an investigative detention of a pedestrian is required for the stop of a vehicle to detain an occupant. A stop of a pedestrian or vehicle may not be conducted randomly or whimsically; it must be based on reasonable and articulable suspicion of criminal activity. Though probable cause is sometimes required to search a vehicle, it is not required to stop one. *Delaware v. Prouse*, 440 U.S. 648 (1979).

Checkpoints

Even stops without any particularized suspicion are lawful under some circumstances. Vehicle "checkpoints," for example, may be permitted in certain regulatory situations, like driver's license and drunk driving checkpoints, truck weigh stations, and border enforcement. However, checkpoints which have as their primary purpose the more general enforcement of the criminal law – like "drug checkpoints" – were outlawed by the Supreme Court in *City of Indianapolis v. Edmond*, 531 U.S. 32 (2000). More recently, the Supreme Court decided that specific information-gathering checkpoints can be lawful and speculated that other checkpoints would be lawful in order to prevent people (terrorists, for example) from entering certain areas and to prevent people (perpetrators) from leaving certain areas. *Illinois v.*

Lidster, 540 U.S. 419 (2004). Also, some courts have held that even though most criminal investigative checkpoints are prohibited by *Edmond*, "fake checkpoints" – signage indicating the impending presence of an in-fact non-existent checkpoint – may be permitted in order to allow police to scrutinize people's driving behavior upon seeing the signage. *See, e.g. United States v. Martinez*, 358 F.3d 1005 (8th Cir. 2004) and *United States v. Williams*, 359 F.3d 1019 (8th Cir. 2004).

Pretext

"Pretextual stops" are those in which the officer's true investigative motives are not reflected in the "objective" basis for the stop. In *Whren v. United States*, 517 U.S. 806 (1996), the United States Supreme Court held that the Fourth Amendment does not prohibit pretextual stops of motor vehicles as long as there is an objectively lawful justification for the stop. For example, the fact that the officer's real motivation for stopping the vehicle was only a "hunch" of drug involvement does not invalidate a traffic stop that is otherwise lawful for, say, an inoperative tail light. An officer's subjective motivation is irrelevant to the Fourth Amendment validity of an objectively lawful (though pretexual) stop. In *Arkansas v. Sullivan*, 532 U.S. 769 (2001), the Supreme Court extended this rule to a pretextual arrest, and in *United States v. Petty*, 367 F.3d 1009 (8th Cir. 2004) one federal appeals court extended it to inventory searches.

"Pretextual stops" are those in which the officer's true investigative motives are not reflected in the "objective" basis for the stop.

In 1996, the Supreme Court ruled that a pretextual traffic stop does not necessarily have to be ended by the words "you're free to leave now" before an officer moves forward with a request for consent to search. The Fourth Amendment test for a valid consent to search is whether the consent is voluntary, and voluntariness is a question of fact to be determined from all of the circumstances. The Supreme Court ruled that "it would be unrealistic to require officers to always inform detainees that they are free to go before a consent to search may be deemed voluntary." *Ohio v. Robinette*, 519 U.S. 33 (1996).

It is not permissible, though, for officers to extend the duration of a pretextual stop in order to investigate a matter for which they do not have reasonable suspicion. *United States v. Stewart,* 213 Fed.Appx. 898 (11th Cir. 2007) and *United States v. Mendez,* 476 F.3d 1077 (9th Cir. 2007). The pretextual stop must be ended, and voluntary contact established, if such investigation is to ensue. See, for example, *United States v. Guerrero-Espinoza*, 462 F.3d 1302 (10th Cir. 2006).

Actions Related To The Stop

At the officer's option, occupants may be lawfully ordered out of the vehicle for reasons of effectiveness and safety.

Once a vehicle is stopped, the ordinary rules of arrest, detention, and search apply, including the frisk and plain view doctrines. At the officer's option, occupants may be lawfully ordered out of the vehicle for reasons of effectiveness and safety. *See Pennsylvania v. Mimms*, 434 U.S. 106 (1977) and *Maryland v. Wilson*, 519 U.S. 408 (1997). An officer may enter a lawfully stopped vehicle to search for a VIN number even though he has no reason to believe or suspect that the car is stolen, provided the VIN number cannot be viewed from outside the vehicle. *New York v. Class*, 475 U.S. 106 (1986). Such an action to determine a VIN number is a reasonable search, though without warrant or probable cause, because:

1. The entry is limited in purpose and scope to discovery of a number as to which there is no reasonable expectation of privacy;
2. The entry is into an area (a vehicle in a public place) in which expectations of privacy are much diminished; and
3. The governmental interest in regulating vehicles and requiring VIN numbers to be readily visible justifies a limited intrusion to assure the presence of a VIN number, and learn what the number is.

Consent To Search

Although consent searches are dealt with elsewhere, applications specific to vehicle situations are re-stated here.

In order to be valid, a consent to a vehicle search must be obtained from someone who has apparent authority to consent and the consent must be given voluntarily. The required justification for a consent search of a motor vehicle is voluntary permission from the apparent owner and/or person in control of the vehicle to conduct the search. A vehicle operator may have a reasonable expectation of privacy even in a rented vehicle and even if that person's name is not on the rental agreement. See, for example, *United States v. Thomas,* 447 F.3d 1191 (9th Cir. 2006). It is not necessary to advise the subject of his right to refuse to consent to the search.

Containers within the vehicle may be searched if it is reasonable to believe that the container is within the bounds of the consent.

The scope of such a search is anywhere in the vehicle that could reasonably be thought to be within the scope of the consent. Containers within the vehicle may be searched if it is reasonable to believe that the container is within the bounds of the consent. Doing damage to the area or item to be searched would generally require explicit permission.

The person consenting to the search may limit his consent to certain areas of the vehicle and may withdraw his consent at any time. If consent is withheld or withdrawn, no warrantless search may be conducted unless it can be justified by one or another of the exceptions to the search warrant requirement. Refusal to consent or withdrawal of consent may not be used as a factual justification for conclusions of reasonable suspicion and/or probable cause. A person's refusal to relinquish a constitutional right may not be used as a basis for police action against him.

Refusal to consent or withdrawal of consent may not be used as a factual justification for conclusions of reasonable suspicion and/or probable cause.

In *Florida v. Jimeno,* 500 U.S. 248 (1991), the United States Supreme Court discussed the theory of consent as it related to the search of a container within the vehicle, stating:

> "Respondent granted [the officer] permission to search his car, and did not place any explicit limitation on the scope of the search. [The officer] had informed respondent that he believed respondent was carrying narcotics, and that he would be looking for narcotics in his car. We think that it was objectively reasonable for the police to conclude that the general consent to search respondent's car included consent to search containers within that car which might bear drugs."

The *Jimeno* case does not hold that every consent to search a motor vehicle extends to every closed container inside. Rather, the consent to search the car will extend only to those closed containers which it is reasonable to believe were included. If the subject is told what the object of the search is and the particular container could be concealing the object of the search, the search is likely lawful given the *Jimeno* decision. In *United States v. Garrido-Santana* 360 F.3d 565 (6th Cir. 2004), a federal appeals court applying *Jimeno* found that searching a gas tank was permissible, given consent to search "the car."

Frisk Of Vehicle For Weapons

Car "frisks" are lawful on essentially the same basis as would allow the frisk of a person.

Car "frisks" are lawful on essentially the same basis as would allow the frisk of a person. A warrantless weapons frisk of the passenger compartment of a lawfully-stopped vehicle is permissible if the officer has reasonable suspicion that a dangerous weapon is immediately accessible within the passenger compartment. The frisk is limited to places in the interior passenger compartment in which a quickly-accessible weapon could be placed or hidden. Once established, authority to frisk the vehicle remains even though the suspect is removed from the car and held nearby. *Michigan v. Long*, 463 U.S. 1032 (1983) is the leading case on frisking a vehicle.

A closed container found in the passenger compartment may be opened and checked for weapons if the contents of the container are immediately accessible to vehicle occupants (i.e., the container could be opened quickly without breakage). The trunk usually may not be searched during a frisk of a vehicle for weapons (because the contents of the trunk normally are not immediately accessible to vehicle occupants) but where the trunk is accessible through a rear seat "fold-down" a frisk of the trunk may be permissible. See, for example, *United States v. Arnold*, 388 F.3d 237 (7th Cir. 2004).

Frisk Of Occupants

The frisk of vehicle occupants is regulated by the general law of frisking – *Terry v. Ohio*, 392 U.S. 1 (1968) and its descendant cases. *Terry* defined a frisk as "a carefully limited search of the outer clothing...to discover weapons..." and indicated that such searches are justified if two conditions are present:

1. Lawful basis for investigative detention; and
2. Reasonable suspicion the suspect is armed and constitutes a potential danger to the officer.

Although a number of state courts, legal scholars, and commentators disagree, it appears that carried articles like handbags and backpacks may be "frisked" upon the same justification as would support a lawful body frisk. Quickly accessible articles and areas within the immediate control of the detainee may be secured and frisked. It does not matter that the item could be moved away from the detainee and thereby secured. In *Michigan v. Long*, 463 U.S. 1032 (1984), the Court made clear that police are not required to "adopt alternate means to ensure their safety in order to avoid the intrusion involved in a *Terry* encounter." *See also United States v. Rhind*, 289 F.3d 690 (11th Cir. 2002) and *United States v. Williams*, 962 F.2d 1218 (6th Cir. 1992) for more recent incarnations of this principle.

Search Incident To The Arrest Of A Vehicle Occupant

If an officer lawfully arrests someone in a vehicle, the officer may conduct a warrantless search of the interior passenger compartment of that vehicle incident to the arrest. Although such a search incident to arrest does not normally permit a search of the trunk, a number of courts have allowed searches of the rear or cargo areas of hatchbacks, station wagons, and SUVs. See, for example, *United States v. Mayo*, 394 F.3d 1271 (9th Cir. 2005). All closed containers found in the passenger compartment may be searched if the container can be opened quickly without damaging it. The question with respect to closed containers is whether the contents of the container were within the immediate control of the arrestee before he was removed from his car. Articles like handbags, wallets, and clothing worn by the arrestee which are associated with the person and move with the arrestee may be searched at the time of or after the arrest.

If an officer lawfully arrests someone in a vehicle, the officer may conduct a warrantless search of the interior passenger compartment of that vehicle incident to the arrest.

Once established, authority to conduct a search incident to arrest continues briefly even though the arrestee has been secured nearby but away from his car (for example, in a nearby police car). *New York v. Belton*, 453 U.S. 454 (1981). A search of a vehicle incident to arrest of an occupant is permissible even when the person to be arrested has stepped out of the car just as the officer is approaching to arrest. *Thornton v. United States*, 541 U.S. 615 (2004). However, searches incident to arrest must be "substantially contemporaneous" with the arrest. *Chimel v. California*, 395 U.S. 752 (1969). In plainer English: The search must occur at the time of, or very soon after, the arrest. But see *United States c. Hrasky*, 453 F.3d 1099 (8th Cir. 2006), where a search incident to arrest was permitted after a subject was detained an hour while an officer decided whether to arrest or issue a citation. Other theories (discussed elsewhere) may authorize the later search of an arrestee and his transported belongings.

The only justification necessary for a search incident to arrest is a lawful arrest. It is not necessary for an officer to demonstrate probable cause or even suspicion that weapons, evidence, or contraband are present. Likewise it does not matter whether the officer feared the arrestee or felt endangered. In *Knowles v. Iowa*, 525 U.S. 113 (1998), the Supreme Court held that mere issuance of a traffic citation, even for an arrestable offense, does not justify a search incident to arrest.

"Carroll" Search (Probable Cause Search)

The Fourth Amendment to the United States Constitution does not require a search warrant for vehicles in public areas and never has, insofar as Supreme Court decisions are concerned.

Many officers have been taught that federal constitutional law requires that, whenever it is practical to do so (i.e., absent an "exigency" or emergency), a search warrant should be obtained before conducting a probable cause vehicle search. In fact, federal constitutional law rarely requires a warrant for a vehicle search. A search warrant is required to search a motor vehicle only when that vehicle is not in a publicly-accessed vehicular area, and then only when exigent circumstances do not justify immediate warrantless action. The Fourth Amendment to the United States Constitution does not require a search warrant for vehicles in public areas and never has, insofar as Supreme Court decisions are concerned.

An officer who has probable cause to believe that contraband or other evidence of a crime is in an apparently operable motor vehicle that is in a public area may conduct a warrantless search of any part of the vehicle that could contain the object of the search. This includes any closed container, locked or unlocked, that could conceal the item to be seized. Public areas of course include public streets and roadways and usually include privately-owned properties which are commonly used by the public for vehicular movement (e.g., shopping center and even apartment complex parking lots).

Even when police have ample opportunity to obtain a search warrant before searching a vehicle in a public area, the Fourth Amendment does not require a warrant. Though there exists a pervasive myth to the contrary, the Supreme Court has never held that a search warrant is necessary to conduct a probable cause search of a vehicle in a public place. Rather, in a long line of decisions beginning with *Carroll v. United States*, 45 267 U.S. 132 (1925), the Court has decided consistently that when a motor vehicle is in a public area it is not subject to the warrant requirement. Motor vehicle privacy rights in public areas are simply not as significant as when the motor vehicle is on private property that is not open to public vehicular access.

The Court has decided consistently that when a motor vehicle is in a public area it is not subject to the warrant requirement.

In two 1985 decisions, the Supreme Court reaffirmed its then six-decade-old unwillingness to extend to vehicles in public areas as much Fourth Amendment privacy protection as is accorded homes and other private areas; it also made crystal clear that warrantless searches of vehicles in public areas do not require proof of exigent circumstances.

In the first of its 1985 decisions on the issue, *California v. Carney*, 471 U.S. 386 (1985), the Supreme Court upheld a warrantless search of a mobile motor home parked in a publicly-accessible parking area and restated that such warrantless searches do not require proof of an emergency or of lack of opportunity to obtain a warrant. According to the Court, such warrantless searches are reasonable (upon probable cause) because of either the vehicle's mobility or the reduced expectation of privacy accorded it. Describing what has become known as the "vehicle exception" to the search warrant requirement, the *Carney* Court stated:

> "Besides the element of mobility, less rigorous warrant requirements govern because the expectation of privacy with respect to one's automobile is significantly less than that relating to one's home or office. Even in cases where an automobile was not immediately mobile, the lesser expectation of privacy resulting from its use as a readily mobile vehicle justified application of the vehicular exception."

In the second of its 1985 vehicle search cases, *United States v. Johns*, 469 U.S. 478 (1985), the Supreme Court made its clearest statement regarding exigent circumstances:

> "A vehicle lawfully in police custody may be searched on the basis of probable cause to believe that it contains contraband, and there is no requirement of exigent circumstances to justify a warrantless search."

Nearly two dozen decisions of the Supreme Court testify that there is a vehicle exception to the search warrant requirement and that it does not depend on exigent circumstances, lack of time to obtain a warrant, or other impracticalities.

Today, nearly two dozen decisions of the Supreme Court testify that there is a vehicle exception to the search warrant requirement and that it does not depend on exigent circumstances, lack of time to obtain a warrant, or other impracticalities in obtaining a warrant. The notion that warrantless probable cause searches of vehicles in public areas require special justification (i.e. beyond probable cause) is simply incorrect. A warrantless "*Carroll*" search may be conducted at the place of the initial contact, or later at a different location. Neither the passage of time nor the relocation of the motor vehicle by officers (even to secure custody) creates a need for a search warrant. *See Florida v. Meyers*, 466 U.S. 380 (1984) and *Michigan v. Thomas*, 458 U.S. 259 (1982). Two late 1990s Supreme Court decisions re-affirm the continued validity of the now eight-decade-old "*Carroll* Doctrine." *Pennsylvania v. Labron*, 518 U.S. 938 (1996) and *Maryland v. Dyson*, 527 U.S. 465 (1999). Also, in 1999, the Supreme Court held that, in the course of a traffic stop where an officer noticed the driver had a syringe in his pocket and he admitted using it to take illegal drugs, an ensuing warrantless search of a female passenger's wallet-type container was lawful under the *Carroll* Rule. *See Wyoming v. Houghton*, 526 U.S. 295 (1999).

If, however, the vehicle to be searched is located on private residential property, the *Carroll* Doctrine does not apply and rules respecting homeplace and curtilage privacy may, and typically would, generate a warrant requirement. *See Coolidge v. New Hampshire*, 403 U.S. 443(1971).

Probable Cause Searches Of Containers Within Vehicles

In 1991, the Supreme Court announced that if probable cause to search exists, a closed container found inside a motor vehicle in a public place may be searched without a warrant just as the motor vehicle itself may be. The only requirement for the search is probable cause to believe that evidence or contraband may be inside that container. This decision reversed a longstanding rule (known as the *Chadwick-Sanders* Rule) that a warrant was necessary to search a closed container which officers had specific probable cause to believe contained evidence or contraband. In that case, *California v. Acevedo*, 500 U.S. 565 (1991), the Supreme Court stated:

If probable cause to search exists, a closed container found inside a motor vehicle in a public place may be searched without a warrant just as the motor vehicle itself may be.

> "Until today, this Court has drawn a curious line between the search of an automobile that coincidentally turns up a container and the search of a container that turns up in an automobile. The protections of the Fourth Amendment must not turn on such coincidences. We therefore interpret *Carroll* as providing one rule to govern all automobile searches. The police may search an automobile and the containers within it where they have probable cause to believe contraband or evidence is contained."

The *Carroll* line of cases, including the *Acevedo* decision, creates a simple, easy-to-apply rule. If an officer has probable cause to believe that evidence or contraband is located inside a moveable motor vehicle which is in a public place, a warrantless search for that contraband or evidence is lawful – even if the probable cause information involves a container.

Inventory Searches

According to the Supreme Court, warrantless inventory searches of impounded motor vehicles serve several important societal interests: They protect the owner's property while it is in police custody; they protect officers against false claims of lost, stolen or damaged property; and they protect the police and community from dangerous instrumentalities. These strong interests make inventory searches reasonable even when there is no reason to believe, or even suspect, that the vehicle contains evidence of a crime, valuables, or hazardous materials.

A warrantless inventory search is permissible if a vehicle has been lawfully impounded and the agency conducting the inventory has a departmental policy requiring inventory searches of all impounded vehicles.

A warrantless inventory search is permissible if a vehicle has been lawfully impounded and the agency conducting the inventory has a departmental policy requiring inventory searches of all impounded vehicles. Generally, the entire vehicle (including the trunk, if it can be opened without damage) may be searched during the inventory. However, the scope of the inventory search is limited to those parts of the vehicle which are likely locations for important or valuable items or any dangerous instrumentality. Any closed container found may be examined pursuant to a departmental policy if the container is a likely repository for important items or dangerous instrumentalities. The guiding principle regarding scope of inventory is its caretaking purpose; neither the vehicle nor any container should be damaged during an inventory search, unless necessary to deal with dangerous instrumentalities.

If contraband is discovered, probable cause to search for more evidence of that crime and other contraband is created and other vehicle search rules become applicable. Evidence of crime and/or contraband which is discovered during a lawful inventory may be seized and used in a resulting criminal trial. The Supreme Court decisions which govern this area are *South Dakota v. Opperman*, 428 U.S. 364 (1976) and *Florida v. Wells*, 495 U.S. 1 (1990).

NOTE: For an inventory search to be lawful, the impoundment (i.e., police-ordered tow) must be lawful. Not every arrest of a vehicle occupant or discovery of evidence justifies an impoundment of a vehicle. Officers should consult local counsel and state law to determine when vehicles may be lawfully impounded. Also, in *Florida v. White*, 526 U.S. 559 (1999) the Court held that the same principles that underlie the vehicle exception to the search warrant requirement also apply to the warrantless seizure of a vehicle, when it itself is evidence or subject to forfeiture.

Summary

In sorting out and applying the various theories of warrantless vehicle search, it is important to keep in mind a basic tenet of the Fourth Amendment – searches must be reasonable. A search is reasonable only when its scope is reasonable, i.e., consistent with its underlying justification. For example, if the justifying theory is suspicion that dangerous weapons might be quickly reached by a suspect, the search may be no more extensive or intrusive than is reasonably necessary to check for weapons which are immediately accessible to the suspect.

If, during a lawful warrantless search, items which are immediately apparent to be evidence of crime are discovered, those items may be seized then and there under the plain view doctrine of warrantless seizure even if they are unconnected to the evidence and/or crime(s) which were the original justification for the warrantless search. Finding some quantity of illegal drugs in a motor vehicle typically establishes probable cause to believe that more drugs are present. See, for example, *United States v. Rosborough*, 366 F.3d 1145 (10th Cir. 2004) where even a drug dog alert to the passenger compartment allowed a probable cause search of the trunk. *But see United States v. Jackson*, 415 F.3d 88 (D.C. Cir. 2005), where finding a stolen tag in the passenger compartment plus the driver didn't have a registration was not probable cause to search the trunk.

One type of warrantless search may lead to justification for another type of warrantless search that will permit an even broader, more extensive search.

It is important for officers to understand each theory of warrantless vehicle search and how far each theory can take the officer conducting the search. One type of warrantless search may lead to justification for another type of warrantless search that will permit an even broader, more extensive search.

CHAPTER 5

FORCED ENTRY INTO PRIVATE PREMISES

Use of force risks, notably including deadly force, increase dramatically when an officer makes nonconsensual entry into a home.

Privacy rights surrounding private premises, particularly homes, are fundamental under our Constitution. Improper police entries into private premises can cause serious civil liability, massive problems with evidence suppression, and even criminal prosecution of officers. Use of force risks, notably including deadly force, increase dramatically when an officer makes nonconsensual entry into a home. Because the risks in this area of policing are so great, this subject should be studied carefully and be fully understood by every law enforcement officer.

Terminology

The term "forcible" (as used in this discussion) simply means without voluntary consent. "Forced entry" may involve kicking doors, breaking locks, splintering wood, shattering glass, or it may not. A forcible entry is any entry which is made without voluntary consent from someone who has the authority to consent. For purposes of this discussion, "private premises" are residential premises – homes. This term includes rental housing, including hotel and motel rooms. While private offices and other private premises are generally protected by the Fourth Amendment in approximately the same fashion as homes, this discussion will focus on forcible (i.e. non-consensual) entries by police into homes.

The General Rules For Searches Of Premises

The general rule is that, to force an entry into a home, a warrant is required. An exception to that rule exists in the case of "exigent circumstances." If an officer is forcing an entry into a home for the purpose of arresting someone thought to be inside, there are two additional legal requirements, whether or not a warrant is used. First, there must be probable cause to arrest the person believed to be inside. Second, there must be reason to believe that the person to be arrested is actually currently present in the private premises being entered. A warrant does not automatically give the officer the right to enter private premises to look around to see if the person to be arrested is present.

Liability Warning

If an officer is executing an arrest warrant he knows nothing about, it is reasonable for him to assume that the warrant is valid unless there is something on the face of the warrant that clearly indicates it is defective. *Malley v. Briggs*, 475 U.S. 335 (1986). However, if the officer is aware of the underlying facts and circumstances which give rise to the arrest warrant, and the officer knows those facts and circumstances do not add up to probable cause to believe a crime has been committed by the person subject to the arrest warrant, the officer should not execute that arrest warrant. Instead, the officer should notify prosecutors and/or the court of the issue and seek guidance. The same is true for a search warrant which an officer has reason to believe is invalid.

Reasonable Belief In Arrestee's Presence

As mentioned, before forcing entry into private premises to arrest, the officer must have a reasonable belief, prior to entry, that the person to be arrested is present at that time in the premises. The Fourth Amendment requires that all search and seizures be reasonable. It is not reasonable to enter and search a home for someone unless there is reason to believe that person to be present. *See Payton v. New York*, 445 U.S. 573 (1980) and *United States v. Clayton*, 210 F.3d 841 (8th Cir. 2000). Though some courts differ, the term "reasonable belief," as used here, is used by most courts to be synonymous with probable cause. *See United States v. Gorman*, 314 F.3d 1105 (9th Cir. 2002), for example.

Before forcing entry into private premises to arrest, the officer must have a reasonable belief, prior to entry, that the person to be arrested is present at that time in the premises.

Exigent Circumstances

There is an exception to the general rule – that a warrant is required to enter a home – in the case of exigent circumstances. Over the years, courts have refined the meaning of the term "exigent circumstances" (in respect to entering private premises) and have made it a stricter and more demanding standard. Some still mistakenly characterize exigent circumstances as any kind of time-critical circumstances. In the past, a common teaching example of "exigent circumstances" might have been "hot pursuit." Today, it is clear that not every hot pursuit involves exigent circumstances. The seriousness of the underlying offense or matter is a major factor in determining whether or not there are exigent circumstances. *Welsh v. Wisconsin*, 466 U.S. 740 (1984). Because the exigent circumstances requirement has become more demanding, and because improper warrantless entries into private premises cause such serious risks to officers and to the public, officers should be especially cautious in this area. Danger alone is not sufficient to furnish exigent circumstances; there must be an associated time criticality that makes getting a warrant impractical. See, for example, *Fisher v. San Jose*, 475 F.3d 1049 (9th Cir. 2007).

The seriousness of the underlying offense or matter is a major factor in determining whether or not there are exigent circumstances.

Entry To Arrest

Clearly, officers may enter private premises without a warrant or consent in order to arrest someone in the premises if:

1. Someone is likely to be killed or seriously injured unless immediate warrantless action is taken; or
2. A serious and/or dangerous criminal offender is likely to escape apprehension and/or prosecution unless immediate warrantless action is taken; and
3. There is probable cause to arrest the person sought; and
4. There is probable cause to believe that the person to be arrested is physically present in the premises at the time of the entry.

Not all crimes or matters are serious enough to present "exigent circumstances." The Supreme Court made clear in *Welsh v. Wisconsin* that the seriousness of the underlying offense is an important factor in determining whether or not there are exigent circumstances. In that case, the Court commented that:

> "...It is difficult to conceive of a warrantless home entry that would not be unreasonable when

the underlying offense is extremely minor.

> "...Application of the exigent circumstances exception in the context of a home entry should rarely be sanctioned when there is probable cause to believe that only a minor offense...has been committed."

In light of the *Welsh* decision, officers are best advised not to force a warrantless entry to arrest unless:

1. The offense is a serious and/or dangerous crime and there is a lack of time to obtain a warrant because the subject is likely to escape or to injure someone; or
2. The arrest process began in a public place and there is an immediate, continuous hot pursuit of the suspect into his home. *United States v. Santana*, 427 U.S. 38 (1976) is authority for the proposition that once an arrest has begun in public the arrestee cannot thwart the arrest by simply beating the officer to a doorway. Also under the *Santana* rationale, some courts will allow an investigative detention in the threshold of a door opened pursuant to an officer's request. *See United States v. Crapser*, 472 F.3d 1141 (9th Cir. 2007). For a contrary result in a case of warrantless threshold arrest, *see McClish v. Nugent*, 2007 WL 1063337 (11th Cir. 2007). Lower courts are divided on the legality of what some call "warrantless threshold snatchings."

Entry To Preserve Evidence

If there is probable cause to believe that critical evidence of a serious and/or dangerous offense is located within private premises and that the evidence is very likely to be destroyed or removed unless immediate warrantless action is taken, the officer may enter without a warrant or consent to secure the premises while awaiting the arrival of a search warrant. See, for example, *United States v. Ruiz-Estrada*, 312 F.3d 398 (8th Cir. 2002). Once the premises are secured, no further search should be conducted unless or until:

1. A search warrant for the premises is on scene; or
2. Consent to search has been obtained; or

3. New or additional emergency circumstances arise necessitating additional warrantless search.

There is some risk of evidence loss virtually every time an officer takes the time to obtain a warrant. This does not mean there are always exigent circumstances.

There is some risk of evidence loss virtually every time an officer takes the time to obtain a warrant. This does not mean there are always exigent circumstances. To the contrary, only the very likely loss of critical evidence in serious cases will create legally sufficient "exigent circumstances." *See United States v. Rubin*, 474 F.2d 262 (3d Cir. 1973) and consider the *Welsh* decision, discussed above.

Crime Scenes

For purposes of this discussion, a "crime scene" is defined as a location where a crime has very recently occurred or been discovered and where there is an apparent need for investigative action and/or emergency services. Examples include homicide scenes, fire scenes, and scenes of burglaries or break-ins. The mere presence of contraband or evidence in private premises does not make those premises a "crime scene" for purposes of this discussion.

Upon arriving at a crime scene in private premises, officers may enter the premises without a warrant or consent in order to:

1. Locate and secure perpetrators; and/or
2. Provide assistance to injured or others requiring emergency assistance; and/or
3. Locate and secure evidence that is likely to be lost or destroyed by the mere passage of time.

Crime scene searches are governed by the same rules that govern other searches of private premises. Once exigencies end, consent or a warrant is required.

Once the actions described in the preceding paragraph are completed, no further search should be conducted unless or until:

1. A search warrant for the premises is on scene; or
2. Consent to search has been obtained; or
3. New or additional emergency circumstances arise necessitating further search.

In *Mincey v. Arizona*, 437 U.S. 385 (1978) and *Michigan v. Tyler*, 436 U.S. 499 (1978), the Supreme Court established the above requirements – that crime scene searches are governed by the same rules that govern other searches of private premises. Once exigencies end, consent or a warrant is required. In *Flippo v. West Virginia*, 528 U.S. 11 (1999), the Supreme Court restated that there is no general crime scene exception to the search warrant requirement.

Other Emergencies

Officers may enter private premises without a warrant or consent if it reasonably appears that such action is urgently necessary in order to:

1. Prevent death or serious physical injury; and/or
2. Provide needed emergency medical assistance; and/or
3. Guard against the imminent threat of substantial property damage. See, for example, *Brigham City v. Stuart*, 126 S.Ct. 1943 (2006).

Such actions are "reasonable" under the Fourth Amendment in view of society's interest in police "community caretaking." *See Cady v. Dombrowski*, 413 U.S. 433 (1973). Other courts allow similar action under what they call an "emergency aid" doctrine. *See United States v. Quezada*, 448 F.3d 1005 (8th Cir. 2006) and *United States v. Martins*, 413 F.3d 139 (1st Cir. 2005). Some courts have suggested that the factual justification requirement for such entries may be less than probable cause. *See United States v. Najar*, 451 F.3d 710 (10th Cir. 2006), *United States v. Bradley*, 321 F.3d 1212 (9th Cir. 2003), and *United States v. Martins*, above. Another federal appeals court, "without recognizing the community caretaking doctrine," says going into a home to get the arrestee a shirt and shoes would not satisfy the doctrine in any event, the governmental interest being insufficient to justify the nonconsensual intrusion. *United States v. McGough*, 412 F.3d 1232 (11th Cir. 2005). But going in a "shot-at" home which was the target of a drive-by shooting was permissible to check human welfare even though there were no signs that anyone was home, according to *United States v. Huffman*, 461 F.3d 777 (6th Cir. 2006). Likewise, a 911 hangup with a no-answer call-back will help justify a warrantless entry under the "emergency aid exception." *United States v. Elder*, 466 F.3d 1090 (7th Cir. 2006).

Such actions are "reasonable" under the Fourth Amendment in view of society's interest in police "community caretaking."

If A Warrant Is Required, What Kind Of Warrant?

If one does not have an exception to the rule, one is left with the rule – that a warrant is required. If there is no consent, no hot pursuit, and no exigent circumstances, a warrant is required. The question then becomes what kind of warrant? The two usual possibilities are arrest warrant and/or search warrant.

If the officer wants to enter a home in which the person to be arrested is merely a visitor and not a resident, a search warrant is required.

If an officer has probable cause to believe that the home to be entered is the arrestee's residence and that the arrestee is present there, an arrest warrant is sufficient and no search warrant is required. *Payton v. New York*, 445 U.S. 573 (1980). If the officer wants to enter a home in which the person to be arrested is merely a visitor and not a resident, a search warrant is required. Such homes are sometimes called "third-party premises." In those cases, if there is no consent, no hot pursuit, and no exigent circumstances, a search warrant is required. *Steagald v. Uni*ted States, 451 U.S. 204 (1981).

Officer-Created Exigencies

Generally, officers may not intentionally cause or create exigent circumstances and thereby avoid the requirement of obtaining a warrant.

Generally, officers may not intentionally cause or create exigent circumstances and thereby avoid the requirement of obtaining a warrant. For example, suppose an officer has probable cause to believe that a person to be arrested is at a particular home. Instead of getting a warrant, though he has time to do so, the officer simply goes to that home, knocks on the door, and announces his presence and purpose. No one comes to the door. Can the officer now avoid the warrant requirement by claiming it is likely the offender will get away and/or destroy evidence if the officer leaves to get a warrant? Does the officer now have exigent circumstances? Most courts say no. See, as examples, *United States v. Coles*, 437 F.3d 361 (3d Cir. 2006) and *United States v. Chambers*, 395 F.3d 563 (6th Cir. 2005). Exigent circumstances must arise in the regular course of events. They cannot be created by an officer and then be made the basis for a warrantless intrusion into a home. See, for example, *United States v. Vega*, 221 F.3d 789 (5th Cir. 2000).

Addresses On Warrants

On many arrest warrants there is an address. That address theoretically is the current address of the person to be arrested. However, in many jurisdictions, the process by which addresses get put on arrest warrants is not particularly reliable. For this reason, it is best that, in deciding that a particular place is currently the residence of a particular person, officers do not rely exclusively on the address on an arrest warrant and instead confirm that address as being the current residence of the person to be arrested. Obviously, this can be done in a number of ways, some as simple as checking with a neighbor or calling the power company or the phone company to see who currently has service at the address.

In many jurisdictions, the process by which addresses get put on arrest warrants is not particularly reliable.

The Knock, Announce And Wait Requirements

As discussed earlier, simply having a warrant does not necessarily clear the way for an immediate entry into private premises. In *Wilson v. Arkansas*, 514 U.S. 927 (1995), the Supreme Court ruled that the Fourth Amendment prohibits a "no-knock" forced entry of private premises unless an exigency exists. In *Richards v. Wisconsin*, 520 U.S. 385 (1997), the Court clarified *Wilson* and held that notice before forced entry is constitutionally-required unless the officer has reasonable suspicion that giving notice would:

Simply having a warrant does not necessarily clear the way for an immediate entry into private premises.

1. Endanger someone; or
2. Be futile; or
3. Inhibit effective investigation.

In *Hudson v. Michigan*, 126 S.Ct. 2159 (2006), the Supreme Court held that officers outside a home who could see that a loud physical assault was occurring inside that home were permitted to enter without a warrant, and without knocking and announcing, to attend to the emergency. The officers had reason to believe that knocking and announcing would be futile. *See also United States v. Musa*, 401 F.3d 1208 (10th Cir. 2005) for another good example of a permissible no-knock entry. The entry and search were for drugs and guns and the suspect had a felony record for violent crimes.

The meaning of "knock" is clear. "Announcing" could mean different things to different people. Normally, if an officer loudly states his or her identity ("Police!") and purpose ("Search Warrant!") the knock and announce requirement has been satisfied. The issue then becomes how long must police wait before making non-consensual entry into the premises. In *United States v. Banks*, 540 U.S. 31 (2003), the Court held that when executing a search warrant for a comparatively small amount of easily disposed of narcotics, a 15- to 20-second wait after knocking and announcing was sufficient before entering the small apartment where they believed a suspect to be present.

NOTE: State law is frequently more demanding than the Fourth Amendment regarding "no-knock" entries.

Protective Sweeps

"Sweeps," like frisks, may not be performed automatically as "routine officer safety precautions."

Protective sweeps involve moving through private premises to determine the presence of would-be assailants and other security threats. In *Maryland v. Buie*, 494 U.S. 325 (1990), the Supreme Court held that "sweeps," like frisks, may not be performed automatically as "routine officer safety precautions." Instead, also like frisks, a (non-consensual) sweep requires at least reasonable suspicion of the presence of a threat in the area(s) to be swept. This suspicion must be articulable and it must be particular. See, for example, *United States v. Moran-Vargas*, 376 F.3d 112 (2d Cir. 2004). A general concern for officer safety based on a speculative possibility of a threat is not enough.

In *Buie,* however, the Court made clear that if an officer is lawfully present in a room, it is permissible to glance into adjacent spaces for security reasons – even if there is no particularized suspicion. *See United States v. Thomas*, 429 F.3d 282 (D.C. Cir. 2005) for a more recent illustration of this principle. Apparently, the working definition of "protective sweep" is a room-to-room search for security threat – not just taking a quick look into areas adjacent to where the officer is working. A sweep is permitted (upon reasonable suspicion of a threat) even when the officer is in the home for reasons other than arrest. *See United States v. Miller*, 430 F.3d 93 (2d Cir. 2005) and *United States v. Gould*, 364 F.3d 578 (5th Cir. 2004) (en banc) as examples. For an example of what is enough factual justification for a sweep, *see United States v. Winston*, 444 F.3d 115 (1st Cir. 2006) and *United States v. Cash*, 378 F.3d 745 (8th Cir. 2004). Where reasonable suspicion of a threat extends to outbuildings or vehicles on the premises, they may be "swept" pursuant to the *Buie* Rule. See, as examples, *United States v. Jones*, 471 F.3d 868 (8th Cir. 2006) and *United States v. Maddox*, 388 F.3d 1356 (10th Cir. 2004).

CHAPTER 6

MIRANDA WARNINGS AND WAIVERS

The Supreme Court decision in *Miranda v. Arizona*, 384 U.S. 436 (1966) has become part of American culture. The *Miranda* decision is derived from the Fifth Amendment which in pertinent part prohibits government and government agents from "compelling" someone to incriminate himself in a criminal proceeding. The *Miranda* decision requires that, in certain situations, police inform (advise) people of certain rights in order to undo some of the inherent coercion in some such situations. The *Miranda* Rule is not offense-specific; it applies the same way to all criminal interrogations, whether they involve felonies or misdemeanors. In *Dickerson v. United States*, 530 U.S. 428 (2000), the Supreme Court held for the first time that the *Miranda* rule is part of the constitutional fabric of the United States and is not merely a technical safeguard. However, in *Chavez v. Martinez*, 538 U.S. 760 (2003), the Court held "mere coercion does not violate the text of the Self-Incrimination Clause absent use of the compelled statements in a criminal case against the witness." The Court then made clear that its decision does "not mean that police torture or other abuse that results in confession is constitutionally permissible as long as the statements are not used at trial."

Intentional <u>Miranda</u> violations (to obtain "strategic" advantages) are prohibited even where the subject is subsequently advised of and waives <u>Miranda</u> rights.

So, a "mere" *Miranda* violation is unlikely to cause a constitutional rights deprivation unless it is coupled with other serious abuse <u>or</u> unless the statements are used at criminal trial against the person whose *Miranda* rights were violated. Intentional *Miranda* violations (to obtain "strategic" advantages) are prohibited even where the subject is subsequently advised of and waives *Miranda* rights. For example, if an investigator chooses to conduct an intentionally illegal ("un-*Mirandized*") custodial interrogation to "get the cat out of the bag" and then takes a "*Mirandized*" version of the same confession, both statements are inadmissible. *Missouri v. Seibert*, 542 U.S. 600 (2004). If the preceding *Miranda* violation is unintentional, a second statement can be saved by the proper use of *Miranda* warning and waiver procedures. *Oregon v. Elstad*, 470 U.S. 298 (1985). *See also United States v. Fellers*, 397 F.3d 1090 (8th Cir. 2005). And where physical evidence is derived from an illegally "un-*Mirandized*" custodial interrogation, that physical evidence may nonetheless be admissible. *United States v. Patane*, 542 U.S. 630 (2004).

NOTE: While the Miranda Rule itself is a federal law principle, it is possible that a state could create, by statute or interpretation of state constitution, stricter "Miranda-type" requirements than exist under Federal law. For example, virtually every state has statutory law governing the interrogation of juveniles. Such law often includes special statutory requirements that go further than the federal Miranda Rule.

The "Custody" Principle

The *Miranda* rule applies only to interrogations which occur in a "custodial" environment.

The *Miranda* rule applies only to interrogations which occur in a "custodial" environment. In *Miranda*, the Supreme Court was concerned that the dynamics of custodial police interrogation create an "inherently coercive environment." The Court therefore designed the *Miranda* rule to help protect a person's Fifth Amendment privilege against compelled self-incrimination in that inherently coercive environment. So the Court in *Miranda* requires that an in-custody suspect be advised of his rights before police interrogation efforts may proceed. Then, the subject can knowingly decide whether or not he or she wishes to assert (invoke) the rights or to waive them. A "waiver" is a voluntary relinquishment (giving up) of known rights.

The Supreme Court believed in 1966 (and apparently still does) that in the inherently coercive circumstances of police custody, a person could easily forget that he has the right to remain silent and to counsel, and therefore a reminder is necessary. This reminder procedure (*Miranda*) has been called a "prophylactic" rule. It is a protective measure that helps shield the subject from the inherent coercion of custodial interrogation.

A pre-*Miranda* decision of the Supreme Court, *Escobedo v. Illinois*, 378 U.S. 478 (1964), resulted in what is today a pervasive myth some call "the focus of suspicion" test. This myth has been furthered by lawyers, judges, and law enforcement officers. The myth has it that, when suspicion has focused on a particular person and/or when questioning has become accusatory in nature, that person has become a suspect in a criminal investigation and *Miranda* warnings are therefore required prior to interrogation.

The Supreme Court has squarely rejected the suspect/focus of suspicion test for <u>Miranda</u>.

The Supreme Court has squarely rejected the suspect/focus of suspicion test for *Miranda*. In *Beckwith v. United States*, 425 U.S. 341 (1975), the Court announced and clearly settled that "custody, not focus of suspicion," triggers the *Miranda* requirements. *Miranda* applies only when there is both custody and interrogation. So, if there is interrogation but no custody, or custody but no interrogation, the *Miranda* rule does not apply. The rule applies only when a person is in custody and is about to be interrogated by someone he knows to be a police officer. *See Illinois v. Perkins*, 496 U.S. 292 (1990).

What Is "Custody"?

Understanding the concept of "custody" is essential to the proper application of the *Miranda* rule. The decision of the Supreme Court in *Berkemer v. McCarty*, 468 U.S. 420 (1984), sets out an inquiry to determine whether or not a person is in custody for purposes of the *Miranda* requirement: Would a reasonable person feel he was subjected to those restraints normally associated with formal arrest? Ten years later, the Court re-stated this definition in *Stansbury v. California*, 511 U.S. 318 (1994).

In *Florida v. Bostick*, 501 U.S. 429 (1991), though a Fourth Amendment "seizure" case rather than a *Miranda* "custody" decision, the Supreme Court made clear that a "reasonable" person is an innocent person. Presumably, an innocent person does not suffer the anxieties (and associated altered perceptions) that a guilty person does. The test for *Miranda* custody is an objective test. Therefore, presumably it does not matter if a guilty person may have felt he was in arrest custody as long as officers did not do or say anything that would cause an innocent person to feel that he was restrained to the degree normally associated with a formal arrest.

As discussed in Chapter 2, the Supreme Court recognizes three forms of officer-citizen contact: Voluntary contact, investigative detention, and arrest. *Miranda* "custody" is most easily explained in terms of these three categories. A "voluntary contact" is consensual. The officer has not said or done anything that would cause a reasonable (innocent) person to feel he was being required to participate in the contact. Obviously, voluntary contacts are not custodial and, therefore, in such contacts interrogation is permitted without *Miranda. Miranda* is simply not applicable. Officers who work carefully and artfully through voluntary (non-custodial) contact can conduct a large percentage of their interrogations of criminal suspects without *Miranda* warnings or waiver requirements.

The second form of officer-citizen contact is the investigative detention or "*Terry* Stop." A *Terry* stop is a limited seizure of a person based on reasonable suspicion that the person is, has been, or is about to be, engaged in criminal activity. The Supreme Court has squarely addressed the question of the applicability of the *Miranda* rule to interrogation during *Terry* stops. In two cases, *Berkemer v. McCarty*, 468 U.S. 420(1984) and *Pennsylvania v. Bruder*, 488 U.S. 9 (1988), the Court has held that *Miranda* warnings are not required for interrogation in a *Terry* stop or investigative detention. Even though an investigative detention is a seizure under the Fourth Amendment and the subject clearly is not free to leave, it is not the type of custody that the *Miranda* rule was designed to cover. Both *Berkemer v. McCarty* and *Pennsylvania v. Bruder* involved roadside interrogation of a detained motorist, but principles derived from those cases are applicable to other kinds of investigative stops based upon reasonable suspicion. When *Terry* stops become very "arrest-like," *Miranda* custody may exist, as explained below.

Even though an investigative detention is a seizure under the Fourth Amendment and the subject clearly is not free to leave, it is not the type of custody that the Miranda rule was designed to cover.

The third form of officer-citizen contact – arrest – is generally synonymous with "custody" for purposes of *Miranda*. An arrest is any seizure of a person that goes beyond the limits of a "*Terry* Stop" or investigative detention. While a "*Terry* Stop" is generally a brief, one-location field contact, an arrest typically involves seizures of longer duration or in which persons are required by officers to move involuntarily from one location to another. Involuntary movement of a seized person from one place to another is a hallmark characteristic of an arrest in the constitutional sense. Use of force or restraints that are lawfully part of some investigative detentions may nonetheless cause a reasonable person to feel he has been subjected to restraints normally associated with formal arrest. While the term "custody" under *Miranda* has much the same meaning as the Fourth Amendment concept of "arrest," *Miranda* "custody" likely includes the more intrusive *Terry* stops in which force, shows of force, and/or physical restraints are used and continued. See, as examples, *United States v. Martinez*, 462 F.3d 903 (8th Cir. 2006) and *United States v. Newton*, 369 F.3d 659 (2d Cir. 2004), both involving a handcuffed detainee.

Intent To Arrest

The Supreme Court's decision in *Berkemer v. McCarty* is perhaps the most important decision ever rendered regarding *Miranda*. It answers almost all of the most difficult questions concerning custody and the application of the rule. *Berkemer* clearly settles *Miranda* questions concerning situations where probable cause to arrest exists prior to the interrogation or is developed during the interrogation. In either case, the officer's uncommunicated intent to arrest has absolutely no bearing or relevance on the question of *Miranda* custody. If the officer has not said or done anything that would cause a reasonable (innocent) person to believe that he is in arrest-type custody, it does not matter that the officer has abundant probable cause and intends to arrest the individual at the conclusion of the interview. What an officer is subjectively thinking or feeling concerning prospects of arrest are irrelevant, as long as they are not communicated to the subject. This remains true even when the suspect is a juvenile. *Yarborough v. Alverado*, 541 U.S. 652 (2004).

The officer's uncommunicated intent to arrest has absolutely no bearing or relevance on the question of <u>Miranda</u> custody.

What Is "Interrogation"?

Even when a suspect is in custody, there is no *Miranda* requirement unless the suspect is exposed to police "interrogation." The Supreme Court did not deliver the modern definition of interrogation until the case of *Rhode Island v. Innis*, 446 U.S. 291 (1980). Interrogation is express questioning or its functional equivalent, words or conduct by police that they should know are reasonably likely to elicit an incriminating response from the suspect. Since words or conduct can constitute interrogation, interrogation can occur without any questions being verbalized.

Since words or conduct can constitute interrogation, interrogation can occur without any questions being verbalized.

For example, suppose an officer places a suspect in a situation in which an incriminating response is very predictable by confronting him with an item of physical evidence from a crime scene (e.g., a robbery surveillance photograph) that ties him to the crime. This would likely be considered police interrogation even though no questions were verbalized. If the suspect is in custody, such "interrogation" would likely require prior *Miranda* warning and waiver. A two-step tactic of showing or describing evidence to a suspect, then giving *Miranda* warnings, may be permissible according to some courts. See, as examples, *United States v. Gonzalez-Lauzan*, 437 F.3d 1128 (11th Cir. 2006) and *Hairston v. United States*, 905 A.2d 765 (D.C.App. 2006).

Miranda applies only to police interrogation. In the case of *Illinois v. Perkins*, 496 U.S. 292 (1990), the Supreme Court held that, if an in-custody suspect does not know his questioner is a police officer, there is no "inherent coercion" potential and *Miranda* does not apply. The reasoning: A person cannot be coerced by police interrogation if he does not know his questioner is a police officer. *Illinois v. Perkins* involved the insertion of an undercover police officer into a jail facility to attempt to elicit incriminating information from a jail prisoner in regard to a crime with which he had not yet been formally charged. [NOTE: The Sixth Amendment right to counsel provides additional legal protection to a person who has been formally charged with a crime. In that case, police are prohibited from deliberately eliciting incriminating evidence in regard to the formally charged offense, unless a valid waiver of Sixth Amendment rights has first been obtained. *See United States v. Henry*, 447 U.S. 264 (1980).]

The *Miranda* Warning

There is no magical written or verbal recipe for *Miranda* warnings. Rather, the *Miranda* rule simply requires that the following "message" be conveyed to anyone who is about to be subjected to custodial police interrogation:

1. You have the right to remain silent;

2. Anything you say can and will be used against you in court;

3. You have the right to talk with a lawyer and to have a lawyer with you during any questioning;

4. If you want a lawyer and cannot afford one, one will be appointed to represent you at no cost to you.

There is not an exact set of words that must be read verbatim in order to convey the Miranda message.

This is one version of a *Miranda* warning. All versions must convey these messages or they will be deemed insufficient. However, there is not an exact set of words that must be read verbatim in order to convey the *Miranda* message. The Supreme Court only requires that the *Miranda* message be conveyed in an understandable way. *California v. Prysock*, 453 U.S. 355 (1981).

The Supreme Court ruled in *Colorado v. Spring*, 479 U.S. 564 (1987), that an officer does not have to inform a person of "all possible topics" or of the nature of the investigation as part of an advice of *Miranda* rights. However, it is not advisable for an officer to deceive the suspect concerning the subject matter of the pending custodial interrogation. While courts generally allow certain kinds of deception by police during interrogation (provided the suspect is mentally competent), the type of deception that must always be avoided is that which could affect the voluntariness of a waiver of rights. For example, a suspect who believed he was being questioned on a misdemeanor matter might waive his rights when, had he known the questioning actually concerned a murder, he instead might have chosen to remain silent and/or to seek legal counsel.

Re-warnings

Lower courts have set out factors to consider in deciding whether a "re-warning" of Miranda rights is necessary following a break in interrogation.

Periodically, questions arise as to when and if *Miranda* "re-warnings" are necessary. The Supreme Court has not addressed this issue, but lower courts have set out factors to consider in deciding whether a "re-warning" of *Miranda* rights is necessary following a break in interrogation:

1. The time span since the last *Miranda* warning;

2. Is the same or a different location being utilized for the interrogation?

3. Is the same or a different officer conducting the interrogation?

4. Are there apparent changes in the suspect's mental or emotional state?

5. Is the same or different subject matter being discussed?

The threshold issue regarding re-warnings is whether the suspect is still aware that his earlier understood *Miranda* rights are still in effect. No one factor will necessarily be conclusive. The greater the uncertainty, the greater the need for a *Miranda* re-warning (and possibly re-waiver). *See United States v. Gell-Iren*, 146 F.3d 827 (10th Cir. 1998) for a modern discussion of this issue, and *United States v. Pruden*, 398 F.3d 241 (3d Cir. 2005) where a 20-hour break in the interrogation did not necessitate a *Miranda* re-warning because all other factors had remained constant (the Court noted this was a "close case").

The *Miranda* Waiver

A *Miranda* warning by itself is legally insignificant. A valid *Miranda* **waiver**, however, allows interrogation to proceed and is of great legal consequence. The significance, then, of giving a *Miranda* warning is that it puts the officer in a position to obtain a valid waiver of those rights. A waiver (in this context) is a voluntary relinquishment of a known right. The *Miranda* warning is necessary to establish this known set of rights.

A waiver of *Miranda* rights does not have to be in writing or even explicit. Any clear expression of willingness to have questioning proceed without a lawyer present may show a waiver.

A typical waiver question is: "Having these rights in mind, are you willing to answer questions now without a lawyer present?" An affirmative response generally shows a voluntary relinquishment of known rights assuming, of course, that no unlawful coercion occurs during this process. A waiver of *Miranda* rights does not have to be in writing or even explicit. Any clear expression of willingness to have questioning proceed without a lawyer present may show a waiver. *North Carolina v. Butler*, 441 U.S. 369 (1979). *See also Burket v. Angelone*, 208 F.3d 172 (4th Cir. 2000) as an example.

The waiver should be obtained before asking any "interrogative" questions of an in-custody subject. "Interrogative" questions are those which fall within the definition handed down in

Rhode Island v. Innis, above. An officer should not begin such questioning until there has been a clear indication that the subject understands his rights and is willing to have questioning proceed without a lawyer. If a suspect's reply is ambiguous, the officer should ask clarifying questions. Some lower courts have held that when a subject who understands his rights responds to interrogative questions, the fact that he is responding (when he knows he does not have to) shows a waiver of *Miranda* rights. This view seems inconsistent with the notion that waiver must precede interrogation. However, courts (and other experts) continue to disagree over this question.

Exceptions To The *Miranda* Requirement

There are generally two situations in which an in-custody suspect may be questioned without Miranda warnings and waiver.

There are generally two situations in which an in-custody suspect may be questioned without *Miranda* warnings and waiver. The first is the "public safety exception" to the *Miranda* rule. In the case of *New York v. Quarles*, 467 U.S. 649 (1984), the Supreme Court made clear that when there is an objectively reasonable need for an officer to protect himself or the public from immediate danger associated with weapons, prompt questioning of the suspect regarding the location of the weapon(s) may occur without a *Miranda* warning and waiver. *See United States v. Reyes*, 353 F.3d 148 (2d Cir. 2003).

Also, standard booking questions may be asked of an in-custody suspect without the need for *Miranda* warnings and waiver, although it is possible to obtain incriminating information from such questions (e.g. nicknames, aliases, home addresses for a subsequent search, etc.). Booking questions are not within the *Miranda* rule because they are not the type of questions that the *Miranda* decision was designed to cover. *See Pennsylvania v. Muniz*, 496 U.S. 582 (1990). *See also Rosa v. McCray*, 396 F.3d 210 (2d Cir. 2005), where the suspect was asked his "real hair color." Booking-type questions may be permitted without *Miranda* even if the booking process is not underway. See, for example, *United States v. Gaston*, 357 F.3d 77 (D.C. Cir. 2004).

Volunteered Statements

"Volunteered" statements are not exactly the same thing as "voluntary statements." To be admissible and trustworthy, all statements – including those resulting from interrogation – must be "voluntary" in the sense that they are not "compelled" by government coercions. Volunteered statements on the other hand, sometimes called "spontaneous utterances," are words or statements from a subject that are not prompted by interrogation. Only custodial interrogation requires a *Miranda* warning and waiver. If a subject is volunteering information without interrogative stimuli, *Miranda* is simply not applicable. The resulting statements are admissible in evidence whether or not *Miranda* warnings were given and a waiver was obtained. The *Miranda* decision itself makes this point clear. In the event that a subject begins volunteering information, officers may simply listen carefully and are not required to interrupt. Short clarifying questions concerning a volunteered statement also may be permissible without *Miranda* warnings or waiver. For example, suppose an in-custody armed robbery suspect spontaneously asks his arresting/transporting officer, "Have you guys found the gun yet?" The officer responds, "What gun are you talking about?" The suspect replies, "You know, my gun, the one from the robbery." [NOTE: This exchange is from a real case.] *See United States v. Rhodes*, 779 F.2d 1019 (4th Cir. 1985) and *United States v. Cordova*, 990 F.2d 1035 (8th Cir. 1993) as other examples.

If a subject is volunteering information without interrogative stimuli, Miranda is simply not applicable.

CHAPTER 7

THE RIGHT TO COUNSEL AND THE RIGHT TO SILENCE

Patrol officers and investigators often want to use, as evidence in criminal trials, statements which were made by the defendant and are incriminating in nature. Whatever the degree to which a defendant's prior statements are incriminating, it is likely that the prosecutor's efforts to use the statements at trial will be met with defense objections, often in the form of pretrial motions to suppress the evidence. When these defense objections and/or motions are argued, often at pretrial suppression hearings, the defense attorney will try to show that the incriminating statements were obtained illegally. If the prosecution cannot prove the contrary, the statement generally may not be used at trial, because of the "exclusionary rule" or "fruit of the poisonous tree" doctrine. The same constitutional rights violations may result in police civil liability as well.

Evidence and liability problems regarding a suspect's incriminating statements usually fall into one or more of four categories.

Evidence and liability problems regarding a suspect's incriminating statements usually fall into one or more of four categories – each involving a claim that the defendant's constitutional rights were violated. They are:

1. The statement was the product of an unlawful Fourth Amendment seizure of the defendant's person – an arrest without probable cause or investigative detention without reasonable suspicion (as earlier discussed).

2. The interrogation did not comply with the *Miranda* rule (as earlier discussed) and/or the associated protections of the rights to silence and counsel, if asserted.

3. The statement was obtained in violation of the defendant's Sixth Amendment right to counsel.

4. The statement was a product of unlawful coercion in violation of the Fifth Amendment protection against compelled self-incrimination and the Fourteenth Amendment requirement that, to be admissible, an incriminating statement must be voluntary.

Although these four claims involve interrelated legal theories, each represents a separate, independent constitutional issue. Each represents a liability threat to police as well as the obvious threat to evidence admissibility.

This discussion focuses on two questions:

1. Whether or not police may attempt interrogation after a person attempts to assert a right; and

2. What procedure must be followed to obtain a valid waiver of a right, if a waiver is required.

Right To Counsel Issues

The right to counsel comes in two varieties. One is the right to counsel created in the *Miranda* decision. This right to counsel is associated with the Fifth Amendment right to remain silent and is designed to help protect a person subject to in-custody interrogation from being compelled to incriminate himself. This Fifth Amendment-based right to counsel is separate and distinct from the better known Sixth Amendment right to counsel.

The right to counsel comes in two varieties.

The differences between the two rights to counsel are important. The Fifth Amendment or *Miranda* right to counsel is present any time there is police interrogation of a person who is in arrest-type custody. The Sixth Amendment right to counsel only arises or "attaches" when formal charges have been brought and protects the defendant from any "deliberate elicitation" of self-incriminating information. The Sixth Amendment right to counsel protects the defendant even in many non-custodial settings and may impose different waiver requirements. Also, rules regarding interrogation after assertion of rights vary according to which right has been asserted.

What Rights Have "Attached"?

Some constitutional rights apply only in certain limited circumstances. A person does not always "own" every constitutional right. For example, a person does not own the Sixth Amendment right to counsel unless and until he is formally charged in a criminal proceeding. When a constitutional right has become applicable in a certain situation, that right has "attached." The significance of attachment is twofold:

1. Once a right has attached, a valid waiver of that right must occur before any interrogation (or, in the case of the Sixth

Amendment right to counsel, "deliberate elicitation") takes place; and

2. Once a right has attached, a suspect may assert that right and thereby impose special additional restrictions on further interrogation efforts by police. It is critical to understand when various rights attach.

When The Right To Silence Attaches

The right to silence is a function of the Fifth Amendment privilege against compelled self-incrimination. For purposes of police interrogations, it should be assumed that every person always has the right to remain silent.

When The Fifth Amendment Right To Counsel Attaches

The Fifth Amendment right to counsel was created by the Supreme Court as part of the *Miranda* rule...The Sixth Amendment right to counsel attaches only when someone is "formally charged" with a crime.

The Fifth Amendment right to counsel was created by the Supreme Court as part of the *Miranda* rule. Because it is a *Miranda* right, it attaches only when a person is in arrest-type custody and is to be interrogated by police. A waiver of this right is therefore unnecessary unless those two conditions (custody and interrogation) occur simultaneously. Arrest alone does not trigger this protection, nor does non-custodial interrogation.

When The Sixth Amendment Right To Counsel Attaches

The Sixth Amendment right to counsel attaches only when someone is "formally charged" with a crime. Formal charging occurs when someone is indicted by grand jury or is "arraigned." Arraignment is a formal, in-court notification to a defendant that he is charged with a particular crime. In many states, this court appearance is commonly referred to by other names, like "preliminary hearing" or "first appearance." Whatever name it goes by, formal charging is generally characterized by the involvement of a prosecutor who brings the charge(s) formally against the defendant, thus marking the commitment of the government to prosecute. Merely taking an arrestee to a magistrate or similar judicial official for jailing or bonding generally is not formal charging, even though the arrestee may be informed by a judicial official of the charges against the arrestee.

What Words Constitute Assertions Of Rights?

The rules regarding interrogation after an assertion of rights vary according to what right is asserted. It is therefore critical that officers listen carefully to the exact words of a suspect as he asserts or attempts to assert rights. Ambiguous statements which resemble assertions of rights may be clarified by questions or discussion concerning the suspect's wishes. Notes and/or recordings should be kept documenting the suspect's exact words, whenever possible.

The rules regarding interrogation after an assertion of rights vary according to what right is asserted.

If a suspect says, "I don't want to talk about this anymore," the right to silence has been asserted. This assertion imposes different restrictions on further interrogation than if the right to counsel had been asserted. A statement, "I'm not sure I want to talk about this, I may need a lawyer," is ambiguous and equivocal. "Can I have a lawyer?" was an unambiguous assertion, says *United States v. Lee*, 413 F.3d 622 (7th Cir. 2005). Only an unequivocal assertion of the right to counsel triggers its protection. *See Davis v. United States*, 512 U.S. 452 (1994) and *Paulino v. Castro*, 371 F.3d 1083 (9th Cir. 2004) (applying *Davis*). Officers may wish to resolve ambiguity by attempts to clarify but federal law does not mandate such efforts.

If An Attached Right Has Been Asserted, What Then?

If an attached right has been asserted, then three questions must be answered:

1. When, if at all, may police later attempt to obtain a waiver and proceed with interrogation efforts?
2. If further interrogation efforts are lawful, what crimes may police bring up for discussion?
3. What, exactly, is necessary for a valid waiver of any rights which have attached?

Assertions Of The Right To Silence

If an in-custody suspect asserts to would-be interrogators the right to silence, that right must be "scrupulously honored."

Michigan v. Mosley, 423 U.S. 96 (1975). This means, at a minimum, that police must at least temporarily stop their interrogation efforts. In *Mosley*, which involved an in-custody assertion of the right to silence, the Court permitted a resumption of police interrogation efforts after Mosley's assertion was "scrupulously honored" for several hours. It may have helped police that, when they resumed their efforts, it was in respect to a different crime.

Assertions Of The Sixth Amendment Right To Counsel

"Deliberate elicitation" obviously includes interrogation but can have much broader meaning and is largely self-defining.

The Sixth Amendment right to counsel prohibits police from deliberately eliciting incriminating information from a criminal defendant in any matter in which he has been formally charged, unless he has validly waived that right. "Deliberate elicitation" obviously includes interrogation but can have much broader meaning and is largely self-defining. In any event, it is "deliberate elicitation" of a formally-charged subject that is prohibited after assertion of the Sixth Amendment right to counsel. *See Fellers v. United States*, 540 U.S. 519 (2004).

Interrogation is, of course, deliberate elicitation. The Supreme Court held in *Michigan v. Jackson*, 475 U.S. 625 (1986), that once the Sixth Amendment right to counsel is asserted at or after formal charging, police are prohibited from further attempts to interrogate regarding the formally-charged matter unless the defendant initiates the communication concerning the case or counsel has been made available to the defendant. Assertions of the Sixth Amendment right to counsel do not block interrogation efforts on matters that are not yet the subject of formal charging, even though factually related. *See Texas v. Cobb*, 532 U.S. 162 (2001) for guidance on this technical issue. An assertion of the Sixth Amendment right to counsel may be valid and binding on police even though the assertion is not made directly to a law enforcement officer. Such assertions often occur at first appearances in court. *See McNeil v. Wisconsin*, 501 U.S. 171 (1991).

The Sixth Amendment right to counsel is separate and distinct from the Fifth Amendment right to counsel created by the Supreme Court in *Miranda v. Arizona*. A defendant has the Sixth Amendment right to counsel only in those matters in which he has been formally charged. In contrast, the Fifth Amendment right to counsel protects a suspect in any custodial interrogation, whether or not he has been formally charged with the matter to be discussed. *See Edwards v. Arizona*, 451 U.S. 477 (1981).

Assertions Of The Fifth Amendment Right To Counsel

Once an in-custody suspect has asserted his Fifth Amendment right to counsel, police are prohibited from all further interrogation efforts on all crimes unless the suspect initiates the communication concerning his criminal involvement or counsel has been made available to the suspect. This rule applies even when follow-up interrogators are completely unaware of the earlier assertion of rights. The burden has been placed on the law enforcement community to devise a system for warning investigators of earlier assertions. *See Arizona v. Roberson*, 486 U.S. 146 (1988).

The burden has been placed on the law enforcement community to devise a system for warning investigators of earlier assertions.

The Supreme Court made clear in *Minnick v. Mississippi*, 498 U.S. 146 (1990), that "counsel has been made available" means counsel must be actually present at any subsequent police-initiated interrogation.

Initiation Of Case Discussion By The Suspect

In all of the above-stated rules, the stated prohibition is of <u>police-initiated</u> efforts to interrogate or otherwise deliberately elicit incriminating information from a suspect who has earlier asserted his rights. If the suspect himself or herself initiates with police new discussion of his or her involvement in the crime at issue, the door is opened for police to resume their efforts at questioning. Depending on circumstances, it may be the case that new warning and waiver procedures are required prior to resumption of such efforts.

What Constitutes A Valid Waiver Of Each Right To Counsel?

The question of what constitutes a valid waiver of *Miranda* rights, the rights to silence and to counsel in custodial interrogations, has been fairly well settled for some time. Officers are familiar with *Miranda* warning and waiver procedures and they are the subject of countless cards, forms, and other writings. Until 1988, however, the Supreme Court had not furnished any significant guidance regarding the requirements for a valid waiver of the Sixth Amendment right to counsel. Lower courts had been divided on the subject, but the Supreme Court decision in *Patterson v. Illinois*, 487 U.S. 285 (1988) cleared the air, holding that a standard *Miranda*-style waiver procedure is sufficient to produce a valid waiver of the Sixth Amendment right to counsel, at least if the suspect is also advised that he has been formally charged with the specific crime that police wish to discuss.

When a person who is not in custody and has not been formally charged voluntarily chooses to talk with police about a matter under investigation, he need not be advised of his rights and a waiver of his rights is implied from his choice to remain with police and talk to them.

Summary

The suspect's rights, and rules concerning them, may come and go as conditions change during investigation and prosecution.

The law regarding attachment, waiver, and assertion of interrogation rights is evolving, growing, and sometimes confusing. More than one right may be in play at any given time. The suspect's rights, and rules concerning them, may come and go as conditions change during investigation and prosecution. Without close attention to these developments, the criminal investigator is almost certain to make dangerous constitutional errors in the interrogation process. The best way to avoid such errors is to consider each of the three possible rights individually and systematically, one by one, in light of the factual situation in a particular case, at a particular time.

In aid of this process, following is a re-statement of the constitutional rules for police dealing with assertions of various interrogation rights.

Assertion Of Right To Silence By In-Custody Suspect

- Cease all interrogation efforts immediately.
- No further interrogation efforts on anything until:

- The suspect has been left alone by police for at least several hours, or
- The suspect initiates new discussion with police of his involvement in criminal activity, or
- The suspect leaves custody.

- If further in-custody interrogation becomes lawful, a waiver of rights, using standard *Miranda* warning and waiver procedures, will still be necessary. (If the suspect is no longer in custody, there is no requirement of a *Miranda* warning and waiver. The suspect's choice to meet and talk with police will show his waiver.)

NOTE: When a suspect who is not in custody chooses to meet with and talk to police, it is clear that he is not asserting his right to remain silent. Therefore, if during non-custodial interrogation a suspect asserts his right to remain silent, police may continue to attempt questioning. The suspect is free not to respond and free to leave, if he wishes. His decision to remain and to respond to further questions indicates his choice to speak with police rather than to assert his right to silence. When an in-custody suspect asserts the right to silence, the assertion must be scrupulously honored.

When a suspect who is not in custody chooses to meet with and talk to police, it is clear that he is not asserting his right to remain silent.

Assertion Of Fifth Amendment (Miranda) Right To Counsel By In-Custody Suspect

- Cease all interrogation efforts immediately.
- No further interrogation efforts on anything until:
  - Counsel is actually present at any subsequent interrogation, or
  - The suspect initiates new discussion with police of his involvement in criminal activity, or
  - The suspect leaves custody.

If further in-custody interrogation becomes lawful, a waiver of rights, using standard *Miranda* warning and waiver procedures, will still be necessary. (If the suspect is no longer in custody, this right is no longer applicable and no waiver of it is necessary.)

NOTE: This protection is a creation of the Miranda rule and applies only when Miranda applies. Miranda rights do not attach unless a person in arrest-type custody is exposed to police interrogation; therefore, they may not be validly asserted in non-custodial interrogation. In a non-custodial interrogation, if the suspect would prefer to consult with a lawyer rather than continue talking to police, the suspect has the option of leaving and going to see a lawyer. The Sixth Amendment right to counsel, if attached, may be validly asserted by persons who are not in custody.

Assertion Of Sixth Amendment Right To Counsel By Formally Charged Suspect

• Cease interrogation regarding the formally charged crime immediately.

• No further interrogation efforts regarding the formally charged crime until:

• Counsel is actually present at any subsequent interrogation, or

• The suspect initiates new discussion with police regarding the formally charged crime.

• If further interrogation becomes lawful, a waiver will still be necessary. A waiver may be obtained by advising the suspect that he has been formally charged with a particular (named) offense, that police wish to discuss the formally-charged matter, then using standard *Miranda* warning and waiver procedures.

The Sixth Amendment right to counsel applies only to matters in which a suspect has been formally charged. Assertion of this right blocks further interrogation efforts only on the formally-charged offense.

NOTE: This right has nothing to do with custody or non-custody. The Sixth Amendment right to counsel applies only to matters in which a suspect has been formally charged. Assertion of this right blocks further interrogation efforts only on the formally-charged offense. Police may still approach the suspect in an effort to discuss uncharged crimes. (Warning: Sometimes a suspect will assert other rights which may protect him from all interrogation efforts during a period of custody.)

A Final Note – "Voluntariness" And Coerced Statements

To be admissible in evidence, an incriminating statement must not only clear the above-discussed hurdles, it must be made "voluntarily" and not be "compelled" by unlawful government coercion. *Schneckloth v. Bustamonte*, 412 U.S. 218 (1973) and *Arizona v. Fulminante*, 499 U.S. 279 (1991). Determination of what is unlawful coercion and when a statement is voluntary tends to involve the interplay of three factors: (1) The conduct of the government agent (interrogator); (2) the susceptibilities of the subject (confessor); and (3) the environment in which the activity (interrogation) occurs.

Some coercions are so extreme and obvious that virtually any resulting statement would be judged involuntary. Physical abuse and/or deprivation, threats and/or promises in exchange for confession, and other extreme forms of will-bending are all likely to fall into this category. See, for example, *United States v. Lopez*, 437 F.3d 1059 (10th Cir. 2006). But consider comparatively innocuous statements like "You'll feel better if you get this off your chest – that's a promise." In fact, within a certain spectrum of government behavior there is a sliding scale of acceptability which depends substantially on the two other factors.

For example, deceptive interrogative tactics like pretending to have evidence which, in fact, does not exist may well be permitted if the suspect is intelligent, criminally experienced, and "used to" playing such games. *Frazier v. Cupp*, 394 U.S. 731 (1969). Used on an inexperienced, mentally challenged juvenile, such deception would almost certainly be impermissible. The susceptibilities of the individual suspect to a particular form of coercion will often decide whether that coercion is legally acceptable. Other "susceptibilities" could include cognitive impairments stemming from drunkenness, drugs, heavy medication, pain, and the like.

The susceptibilities of the individual suspect to a particular form of coercion will often decide whether that coercion is legally acceptable.

Similarly, the environment of the interaction will significantly influence whether certain level and types of coercion will be permitted on certain types of suspects. Perhaps the most coercive environment is police custody – because any coercion is inescapable. In fact, the Supreme Court's reason for creating the *Miranda* rule was the "inherently coercive" effect of police custody. As a single factor, of course, custody does not render a derivative statement involuntary.

Determining "voluntariness" involves a few absolutes and many variables.

In any event, determining "voluntariness" involves a few absolutes and many variables. Telling someone that, if he confesses, he will receive a lighter sentence or no imprisonment is too much. Telling someone "I don't make the deals, the prosecutor does. If you cooperate, I'll make sure the prosecutor knows it" is usually permitted. Like many other areas of police law, legal determinations of voluntariness are heavily fact dependent. See, for example, *McCalvin v. Yukins*, 444 F.3d 713 (6th Cir. 2006).

CHAPTER 8

SEARCHES OF PERSONS

Searches of persons involve substantial risks, physical and legal, to the law enforcement officer. They also involve some of America's most valued freedoms. The following discussion will address the following constitutional issues: (1) When and if a frisk search is permitted; (2) the permitted extent and limit of a lawful frisk search; (3) when and if a search incident to arrest is permitted; (4) the permitted extent and limit of a search incident to arrest; and (5) inventory search rules and procedures.

Frisk Searches

The landmark case dealing with frisk searches is the Supreme Court decision in *Terry v. Ohio*, 392 U.S. 1 (1968). In *Terry*, the Court defined an officer's authority to conduct a limited search of a person for weapons during some investigative detentions, or "stops." For such a weapons "frisk" to be reasonable (and constitutional under the Fourth Amendment) the preceding seizure of the subject's person (the stop) generally must be lawful and there must be an objectively reasonable basis for the frisk itself.

A frisk is a limited search of outer clothing (and sometimes carried belongings) for weapons. The main purpose and justifying theory of a frisk search is officer protection. The Supreme Court has characterized the frisk as a "search" because it constitutes an intrusion upon a person's reasonable privacy expectations. The Court has recognized that it is sometimes reasonable for an officer to conduct a protective search for weapons even when the officer does not have probable cause to arrest.

The Court has recognized that it is sometimes reasonable for an officer to conduct a protective search for weapons even when the officer does not have probable cause to arrest.

Just as an investigative stop must be supported by articulable circumstances that establish reasonable suspicion of criminal activity, a frisk must be supported by an articulable reasonable suspicion that a person (lawfully stopped) is armed and constitutes a threat to the officer. As is true also for stops, reasonable suspicion to conduct a frisk may be based on the officer's own knowledge and personal observations (plus reasonable inferences which training and experience allow) or from reasonably reliable information supplied by others. Information from anonymous sources is not considered reliable without additional indicators of credibility. In *Florida v. J. L.*, 529 U.S. 266 (2000), the Supreme Court held that an anonymous tip that a particular person at a particular place is carrying a gun is not, without more, sufficient for reasonable suspicion to stop and frisk.

Suspicion Factors For Frisk Searches

The justification for an investigative stop is not necessarily also justification for a frisk. In each case, an officer conducting a frisk must be prepared to point to the specific, articulable facts that justified that particular frisk. Possible justifications (or factors) for a frisk search include:

Specific Information

Information received from witnesses or other sources may suggest that a person is armed. Even anonymous source information may be considered if circumstances indicate reasonable trustworthiness of the information. *But see Florida v. J. L.*, above.

Visual Observations

Observation of certain bulges in a suspect's clothing that are consistent with the likely presence of weapons may suggest just that. Typically, the observation of such a bulge in a suspect's clothing will be sufficient by itself to justify a protective frisk during a lawful stop.

Although the reasonable suspicion that justifies an investigative stop does not automatically justify a frisk, in some instances the very nature of the suspected criminal activity may suggest the presence of weapons.

Nature Of The Suspected Criminal Activity

Although the reasonable suspicion that justifies an investigative stop does not automatically justify a frisk, in some instances the very nature of the suspected criminal activity may suggest the presence of weapons. For example, officers normally would be justified in conducting a frisk of a person stopped on reasonable suspicion of armed robbery. The potential presence of weapons is reasonably inferred from the nature of the suspected criminal activity. In some areas, the same may be true in regard to street-level drug dealers.

Discovery Of Weapons

When an officer observes a weapon in the vicinity of a person who has been lawfully stopped, the officer may reasonably suspect that other weapons are present and pose a threat. It is usually reasonable for an officer to take preventive measures to ensure that there are no other weapons within the person's reach.

Officer Knowledge Of Area And/Or Groups

Officers often have considerable knowledge and/or experience regarding certain places and/or groups. Example: An officer stops a person coming out of an illegal nightclub well known for its armed patrons.

Suspect Behavior

Suspicious movements and other non-verbal behavior may sometimes be a basis for suspecting that weapons are present.

Suspicious movements and other non-verbal behavior may sometimes be a basis for suspecting that weapons are present. The failure to comply with an officer's command to remove one's hand from a pocket might reasonably cause suspicion that a weapon is present. Extreme suspect nervousness may count toward reasonable suspicion of the presence of weapons in some situations. *But see United States v. McKoy*, 428 F.3d 38 (1st Cir. 2005), where a motorist was stopped in the daytime, for a parking violation in a "high-crime" area, was nervous, avoided eye contact, and twice leaned toward the center console, was not enough for a frisk. This specific case result is likely an effort by a court to make a statement: To remind that a number of behaviors that could point to the possible presence of weapons may be also consistent with ordinary citizen behavior in a contact with police and that frisk searches are not automatically justified by nervous behavior. This particular problem might have been solved for police by expanded articulation of training and experience – and consequent suspicion.

The frisk of a person may not go further than is necessary to accomplish its purpose.

Scope And Nature Of The Frisk Search

The frisk of a person may not go further than is necessary to accomplish its purpose. The sole object of a frisk is to determine whether a weapon is present and to neutralize the threat of physical harm to the officer and others. Therefore, the scope of the frisk is limited to the area from which weapons could be immediately accessed. Quick accessibility is the key concept in determining the scope of a frisk search. Generally this concept implies that no damage or breakage be done to carried belongings or containers. Generally, if one has to break open a container to reach its contents, those contents would not be considered immediately accessible. Reaching into the instep of a high top tennis shoe is permissible as part of a frisk search, according to *United States v. Barboza*, 412 F.3d 15 (1st Cir. 2005).

Manipulation of clothing and objects is allowed only to the extent necessary to confirm or dispel suspicion that an object is a weapon.

Manipulation of clothing and objects is allowed only to the extent necessary to confirm or dispel suspicion that an object is a weapon. Once a determination is made by the officer that the object is not a weapon, manipulation of that object (as part of a frisk search) must immediately cease, but the officer is not required to ignore sensory perceptions gained prior to that moment – the feel of drugs for example. *Minnesota v. Dickerson*, 508 U.S. 366 (1993). *See also United States v. Bustos-Torres*, 396 F.3d 935 (8th Cir. 2005), where the officer felt "wads of cash" during a weapons frisk of a suspected street drug dealer.

If, during lawful frisk activity, an officer feels something that is likely to be contraband or other evidence of crime the officer may attempt to obtain consent from the person to retrieve the item or the officer may proceed under a different search theory, if available (probable cause theory, for example). Pursuant to frisk authority, the officer may remove any item or object that he reasonably believes to be weapon. If the object or item removed is not a weapon but is immediately apparent to be evidence of a crime, it may be seized under the plain view doctrine of warrantless seizure (discussed in a later section).

The "Plain Feel" Doctrine

An officer is not required to ignore what the officer perceives through the sense of touch.

As mentioned earlier, an alternative theory that justifies many search and seizure actions is "probable cause." An officer is not required to ignore what the officer perceives through the sense of touch. *See Minnesota v. Dickerson*, above. This "plain feel" concept is consistent with the general principle that probable cause may be based, in whole or in part, on the sensory perceptions of an officer as interpreted in light of the officer's training and experience. Therefore, if an officer touches an object during a lawful frisk search, determines that the item is not a weapon but perceives through the sense of touch that the item likely is contraband, the officer may make a warrantless seizure of that item based upon probable cause. The legal theory justifying this warrantless intrusion may be either exigent circumstances or search incident to arrest.

Exigent Circumstances And Searches Of Persons

With respect to possession of contraband, the same probable cause that could be used to obtain a search warrant usually would also form the basis for a probable cause arrest and associated search incident to arrest.

"Exigent circumstances" is a clearly-established exception to the search warrant requirement and may be used in situations where an officer has probable cause to believe that a person located in a public place is in possession of contraband or other evidence of crime. In such circumstances, a warrantless, probable cause based, exigent circumstances search would be lawful because of the inherent mobility of the evidence and the likelihood it would be gone (along with the suspect) if the officer left to obtain a search warrant. See, for example, *United States v. Banshee*, 91 F.3d 99 (11th Cir. 1996). If the suspect was detained while a warrant was sought, the time passage involved usually would render the detention an arrest by the time a warrant was delivered to the detention scene. So to detain the subject for the time necessary to obtain a search warrant would almost always amount to an arrest in any event. Fortunately for police, with respect to possession of contraband, the same probable cause that could be used to obtain a search warrant usually would also form the basis for a probable cause arrest and associated search incident to arrest. Either exigent circumstances or search incident to arrest would furnish the warrantless search justification in such situations.

NOTE: the term "exigent circumstances" has different (and less demanding) meaning here and in vehicle searches than it does in connection with entries and searches of homes.

Search Incident To Arrest

The landmark Supreme Court decision on search incident to arrest is *Chimel v. California*, 395 U.S. 752 (1969). A search incident to arrest is permitted automatically pursuant to every lawful arrest. The search incident to arrest must be conducted "substantially contemporaneously" with the arrest but may precede announcement of arrest. *Rawlings v. Kentucky*, 448 U.S. 98 (1980); *see also United States v. Smith*, 389 F.3d 944 (9th Cir. 2004) and *United States v. Powell*, 2007 WL 1119641 (D.C. Cir. 2007) (en banc)for recent applications of this principle.

A search incident to arrest is permitted automatically pursuant to every lawful arrest.

Probable cause to arrest is required for a search incident to arrest, but the search may be conducted whether or not there is any reason to believe evidence and/or weapons will be found. *United States v. Robinson*, 414 U.S. 218 (1973). In *Knowles v. Iowa*, 525 U.S. 113 (1998), the Supreme Court held that issuance of a traffic citation (even for an arrestable offense) does not justify a search incident to arrest. A custodial arrest must be in progress before there can be a search incident to arrest. At least one federal appeals court has limited the *Knowles* rule to traffic citations and allowed a "search incident to citation" of a pedestrian. *United States v. Pratt*, 355 F.3d 1119 (8th Cir. 2004). However, there is no trend supporting the approach taken by the *Pratt* court.

Scope And Nature Of Search Incident To Arrest

A search incident to arrest is a full and complete search for evidence and weapons within the area of immediate control of the arrestee, although damage or breakage generally is not permitted. The search may extend to the person, his/her clothing and carried belongings, and other areas within the immediate control of the arrestee. Example: If the arrest occurs in a motel room, a search incident to arrest may be conducted of the area immediately surrounding the arrestee. This may include looking in drawers, closets, under furniture, and in other places that could have been quickly reached by the arrestee. See, for example, *United States v. Currence*, 446 F.3d 554 (4th Cir. 2006), where a search incident to arrest properly included taking the handlebar caps off of the bicycle the arrestee was riding.

In the event that an arrestee wants or needs access to particular areas for his or her convenience and/or comfort, the officer may inform the arrestee that such access is conditional upon the arrestee's consent to a prior search by the officer of the areas to which access is requested. *Washington v. Chrisman*, 455 U.S. 1 (1982). If consent is withheld, the arrestee normally would be denied access to that particular area. Subsequent access to toilets and such then would be allowed in facilities where the subject did not have a reasonable expectation of privacy – public facilities, for example – where the officer could conduct a prior search of the area to be accessed by the arrestee.

Motor Vehicles And Searches Incident To An Arrest

If the arrestee is seized from within a motor vehicle, the search incident to arrest may extend to the accessible portions of the passenger compartment even if by the time of the search the arrestee has been removed from the vehicle and secured nearby. *New York v. Belton*, 453 U.S. 454 (1981). This is discussed more fully in Chapter 4, Vehicle Stops and Searches at page 41.

Search Incident To Change Of Custody

A search incident to arrest is also authorized upon a change of custody, consistent with the Fourth Amendment's requirement that searches and seizures be reasonable. It is reasonable that the police officer acquiring custody of an arrestee be allowed to insure that his prisoner does not have a weapon and/or evidence hidden on or around him, even if another officer may have conducted an earlier search incident to arrest. *See United States v. Avila-Dominguez*, 610 F.2d 1266 (1980), for example.

Full strip and/or body cavity searches are rarely allowed except pursuant to specific orders in search warrants or in certain jail intake procedures.

Strip Searches/Body Cavity Searches

Full strip and/or body cavity searches are rarely allowed except pursuant to specific orders in search warrants or in certain jail intake procedures. See, for example, *Way v. County of Ventura*, 445 F.3d 1157 (9th Cir. 2006). Strip searches and visual body cavity inspections should be reserved for truly exigent circumstances involving high levels of probable cause to believe that weapons and/or critical evidence of serious crimes are present and that the only means reasonably available to remove the threat of access by the arrestee is to conduct such a search. In such cases, the officer should make every reasonable effort to maximize the personal privacy of the arrestee. The search should be conducted by an officer of the same gender as the arrestee, if reasonably possible. Partial strip searches, which involve manipulation of clothing without causing nudity, tend to be effective substitutes for full strip searches.

Body cavity intrusions are authorized only upon very high levels of focused probable cause to believe a weapon or evidence of crime is concealed in the body cavity. Absent consent or dire exigent circumstances compelling immediate warrantless action, body cavity probes should be performed pursuant to a search warrant and only by qualified medical personnel. A visual inspection of the inside of the mouth probably would not be considered a cavity probe.

Search And Inventory Of Personal Possessions Of A Person In Custody

The Supreme Court has made clear that it is reasonable to inventory the carried possessions of a person upon his or her entry into a detention facility. The primary justification for this action is the caretaking responsibility of law enforcement agencies in regard to the valuables and possessions of arrestees. The inventory assures that valuables are identified and safeguarded and helps protect against claims of theft or mismanagement of property. Lastly, the inventory protects officers and the detention facility against introduction of dangerous instrumentalities (bombs, toxic materials, etc.). In order for an inventory search to be lawful, the arrest and commitment into the detention facility must be lawful and there must be departmental policy requiring such an inventory. A leading Supreme Court decision in this area is *Illinois v. Lafayette*, 462 U.S. 640 (1983). In *United States v. Edwards*, 415 U.S. 800 (1975), the Supreme Court held that a

The inventory assures that valuables are identified and safeguarded and helps protect against claims of theft or mismanagement of property.

"second look" at areas and/or items previously searched may be permitted during continuous custody.

CHAPTER 9

NON-SEARCHES: OPEN FIELDS AND WOODS, AND ABANDONMENT

A "search" is an intrusion upon a "reasonable expectation of privacy." For a privacy expectation to be "reasonable," it must be one that society recognizes as such. So an individual person might subjectively feel an expectation of privacy but not have one objectively, because under the circumstances it would be objectively unreasonable.

Police actions that do not intrude on reasonable privacy expectations (or possessory interests in property) are neither search nor seizure and do not implicate the Fourth Amendment.

Police actions that do not intrude on reasonable privacy expectations (or possessory interests in property) are neither search nor seizure and do not implicate the Fourth Amendment. Some such actions involve the type of "looking around" by police that in lay definition would be called "searches"; however, in the Constitutional sense they are "non-searches" because they do not intrude upon reasonable privacy expectations.

Open Fields And Woods

The best way to discuss the concept of "open fields and woods" may be to study a fact situation. Suppose a person buys a 100-acre plot of land and builds a house in the middle of the land in a grove of trees. He then surrounds the property with a barbed wire fence, the type normally used to keep farm animals contained. This person then posts "no trespassing" signs every 25 feet, all the way around the property. A gate is placed on the driveway; the gate has openings on each side which will allow people to enter but keep farm animals inside.

Under these circumstances many people would feel a subjective expectation of privacy in regard to the interior portions of this acreage. However, there is no constitutionally-protected privacy expectation in the property except for that portion of the property which immediately surrounds the home. The Supreme Court has held that the outlying areas are "open fields and woods" despite fencing and other barriers. The "no trespassing" signs may create a criminal or civil obligation but they do not create a reasonable expectation of privacy protected by the Fourth Amendment. *See Oliver v. United States*, 466 U.S. 170 (1984) and, for background, *Hester v. United States*, 265 U.S. 57 (1924).

The area that immediately surrounds the home is called the "curtilage." This concept contrasts with that of "open fields and woods." Curtilage typically receives Fourth Amendment privacy protection but "open fields and woods" do not. Consequently, one must understand where one ends and the other begins.

Curtilage normally equates to the "yard." Not all farmland would be considered the yard of the farmhouse even though the farmland surrounds the farmhouse. Privacy interests inside one's home receive the maximum protection of the Fourth Amendment. The area immediately surrounding the home (curtilage) gets privacy protection that is similar but not identical. Areas surrounding buildings that are seldom-used, non-dwellings within open fields and woods are not protected in the same ways. See, e.g. *United States v. Barajas- Avalos*, 377 F.3d 1040 (9th Cir. 2004).

Privacy interests inside one's home receive the maximum protection of the Fourth Amendment. The area immediately surrounding the home (curtilage) gets privacy protection that is similar but not identical.

When a law enforcement officer walks onto private rural property, perhaps through a gate, passing through open fields and woods toward a residence, he will reach a point where a curtilage begins. An intrusion upon or into the curtilage may be considered a search and therefore may require Fourth Amendment justification, such as probable cause, a search warrant, exigent circumstances, or consent. Several factors are considered when determining if portions of a property are curtilage:

Proximity to the home: The closer the area is to the home, the more likely it is to be curtilage.

Enclosures associated with the home: Privacy screens, interior fences or thick bushes, often define the yard and are often indicators of curtilage.

Nature and use of the area: If the area (or outbuilding) is used for purposes normally associated with family life, such as a garage or carport where the family car is normally parked, the area is likely to be curtilage. *United States v. Dunn*, 480 U.S. 294 (1987).

Not all intrusions onto a curtilage intrude upon reasonable privacy expectations. The use of common entranceways such as driveways or walkways to go directly to a front door usually does not violate a reasonable expectation of privacy. These are the entranceways used by those who would go to the door to knock or deliver packages or mail for example. Because they are commonly used, it would be unreasonable to expect privacy in regard to visual or other sensory observations from those pathways. See, for example, *United States v. French*, 291 F.3d 945 (7th Cir. 2002). Some courts have held that it is permissible for officers to go into a backyard to knock on a back door where they are responding to a call, the home is apparently occupied, but no one responds to the officer's knocking at the front door. See, for example, *Hardesty v. Hamburg Township*, 461 F.3d 646 (6th Cir. 2006).

A nonconsensual entry into a secure building within open fields and woods is likely to be considered a search.

A nonconsensual entry into a secure building within open fields and woods is likely to be considered a search. *See United States v. Pennington*, 287 F.3d 739 (8th Cir. 2002). However, if the windows or door were left open it would not be a search to look into the interior of a barn through those openings. However, looking through an open back door of a home from inside the fenced-in back yard would be a search because there is a reasonable expectation of privacy within the curtilage that protects against such a visual observation. *See Dunn*, above, and *Daughenbaugh v. City of Tiffin*, 150 F.3d 594 (6th Cir. 1998).

The concepts of open fields and woods and curtilage are not hard and fast absolutes and must be considered in light of the totality of the circumstances. Ultimately, resolution involves a common-sense judgment as to which concept applies to the area in question and as to the reasonableness of any expectation of privacy. Unfortunately, the law in this area is not crystal clear or entirely logical.

Abandoned Personal Property

"Abandoned" property is not protected by the Fourth Amendment because it does not involve a reasonable expectation of privacy. The signs of property being abandoned are often matters of common sense. When property is discarded, thrown away, left unattended, unprotected and exposed to the public, it often becomes unreasonable to expect privacy in regard to that property. Such a forfeiture of one's reasonable expectation of privacy is an abandonment. Once property is abandoned, it is not a search for a law enforcement officer to inspect it, and no Fourth Amendment justification is required.

Abandonment Of Residential Property

In general, residential property is abandoned only if it is clearly unoccupied and shows obvious signs of non-use, such as broken windows, open doors, no power connections, etc. Usually, in such circumstances there would be no reasonable expectation of privacy in the property.

In general, residential property is abandoned only if it is clearly unoccupied and shows obvious signs of non-use, such as broken windows, open doors, no power connections, etc.

Where a person has rented a hotel or motel room but check-out time has come and gone, so has his reasonable expectation of privacy, according to *United States v. Kitchens*, 114 F.3d 29 (4th Cir. 1997) and several other cases. This rule might not apply where a person has merely held his room a few hours beyond the required checkout time or where there exists a practice of allowing guests to "stay-over." *See United States v. Dorais*, 241 F.3d 1124 (9th Cir. 2001). For an apartment (or other longer-term rental property) to be considered abandoned, the renter must have clearly vacated the apartment or been evicted by lawful authority and process. See, for example, *United States v. Hoey*, 983 F.2d 890 (8th Cir. 1993).

Abandonment Of Vehicles

The Fourth Amendment concept of abandonment is not necessarily the same as "abandoned vehicles" under state and local laws allowing removal of vehicles for reasons of public health, safety, or aesthetics. The signs of abandonment in the constitutional sense are much like those discussed above regarding residential property. The location of the vehicle will often be a guiding factor. For example, in *United States v. Gillis*, 358 F.3d 386 (6th Cir. 2004), a federal appeals court found no reasonable expectation of privacy in a wrecked and unlocked vehicle in a driveway but so close to the street that anyone walking down the street could have easily reached into the car. *See United States v. Ramirez*, 145 F.3d 345 (5th Cir. 1998), for a general discussion of these issues.

Trash, Garbage, And The Abandonment Rule

When trash has been placed in a public area for pick up, a reasonable expectation of privacy no longer exists.

When trash has been placed in a public area for pick up, a reasonable expectation of privacy no longer exists. When a person who lives in an apartment complex puts his garbage into a plastic bag, carries that bag to the common dumpster and deposits it inside, the contents of the bag thereafter may be inspected without Fourth Amendment implications because there is no longer a reasonable expectation of privacy in the contents of the bag. The garbage bag is abandoned and the inspection of the contents would not be a search. *California v. Greenwood*, 486 U.S. 35 (1988). When a trash can is placed for pickup on the curb next to the street (although still on the curtilage) it generally becomes unreasonable to expect privacy in its contents. *See United States v. Bowman*, 215 F.3d 951 (9th Cir. 2000). The contents would be considered abandoned. However, a trash can located next to the house and not yet "put out" by the street, may still involve a reasonable expectation of privacy. Examination of the contents would be a search requiring consent or other Fourth Amendment justification. *But see United States v. Segura-Baltazar* 448 F.3d 1281 (11th Cir. 2006), where the Court held that such an expectation of privacy no longer existed after sanitation workers picked up the trash at a regularly-scheduled time.

NOTE: This is an area where a number of states have created state law that is more restrictive than the federal principles stated above.

Abandonment By Verbal Or Non-Verbal Interaction

Suppose an officer who suspects that a person may be transporting cocaine in a briefcase simply walks up to that person and asks him if the briefcase is his. The person says the briefcase is not his, places it on the ground, and walks away from it. The officer calls out, "Do you know whose it is?" The person responds, "It's not mine and I don't know whose it is." The officer may now open the briefcase without a search warrant or other Fourth Amendment justification because the possessor has voluntarily relinquished any once-held reasonable expectation of privacy. The briefcase is abandoned. *See United States v. Sanders*, 130 F.3d 1316 (8th Cir. 1997), for example. State appeals courts often find no abandonment on similar facts.

For such an abandonment, there must be an affirmative denial of ownership and possessory interest. If that occurs, and if the object is located in an area where there is no other reasonable expectation of privacy, the object may be opened and inspected without satisfaction of Fourth Amendment requirements. In those situations where the totality of circumstances suggests that someone else may have a reasonable expectation of privacy in the item in question, special care must be taken to ensure that any abandonment comes from the right person or persons. Although the bag may be near one person, the bag may actually belong to someone else standing nearby or someone who is not present at all. For example, society would generally recognize an ongoing reasonable expectation of privacy in luggage that is still within the control and caretaking function of a common carrier such as a bus company – even if the item has been placed in a luggage retrieval area and persons nearby disclaim interest in the item. *See United States v. Garzon*, 119 F.3d 1446 (10th Cir. 1997). Of course, where someone clearly discards or intentionally leaves behind an item in a public area, it is abandoned. *See United States v. Liu*, 180 F.3d 957 (8th Cir. 1999).

Society would generally recognize an ongoing reasonable expectation of privacy in luggage that is still within the control and caretaking function of a common carrier, even if the item has been placed in a luggage retrieval area and persons nearby disclaim interest in the item.

CHAPTER 10

NON-SEARCHES: THE PLAIN VIEW DOCTRINE, SENSORY PERCEPTION AND ENHANCEMENT TOOLS

A "search" is a governmental intrusion upon a reasonable expectation of privacy. A search may or may not involve a physical intrusion. It may occur without entering any private premises or touching any person or property. A search might be the utilization of a bugging device to hear a private conversation, the use of an unlikely vantage point to gain a visual observation, or the use of intrusive technology not in common public use. A search is a government intrusion upon a concept – the reasonable expectation of privacy.

The Supreme Court has developed a two-part test for whether a privacy expectation is reasonable under the Fourth Amendment:

1. Did a person actually, in fact, expect privacy?
2. Does society recognize that person's expectation as being reasonable and legitimate?

In *Katz v. United States*, 389 U.S. 347 (1967), the Supreme Court stated a fundamental legal principle:

> "What a person knowingly exposes to the public even in his own house or office is not the subject of Fourth Amendment protection."

Law enforcement officers are permitted to take advantage of this principle in order to facilitate criminal investigations, but there are rules. Following is a discussion of the most important of them.

The Plain View Doctrine

The "plain view doctrine," widely misunderstood and misused, is better described as the "plain view doctrine of warrantless seizure."

The "plain view doctrine," widely misunderstood and misused, is better described as the "plain view doctrine of warrantless seizure." For purposes of this discussion, the term "seizure" is defined as a significant (meaningful) interference by government with a person's possessory interest in property. The plain view doctrine of warrantless seizure deals not just with seeing things, but with seizing them. Just because an officer can see an item doesn't mean an immediate warrantless seizure is permitted. The plain view doctrine of warrantless seizure may be stated as follows:

An officer lawfully present in a given location who sees in plain view an item which is immediately apparent to be evidence of a crime may seize that item without a warrant provided no further intrusion upon a reasonable expectation of privacy is required in order to accomplish the seizure.

Example: Suppose an officer walking down a common corridor outside a row of motel rooms looks into an uncurtained window and sees illegal drugs and related paraphernalia on a table. Most would agree that there is a reasonable expectation of privacy within a motel room; however, there is no reasonable expectation of privacy in what one knowingly exposes to the public. The question then becomes, "Is the room occupant knowingly exposing his activity in that room to public view?" In this case, the answer is "yes." Therefore, it is not a search for a police officer to stand outside and look inside. This sensory perception is a "non-search"; it is often called a "plain view observation" but it does not involve the plain view doctrine of warrantless seizure.

The plain view doctrine of warrantless seizure has to do with seizing items, not just seeing them. When only seeing is involved, there is only one pertinent constitutional question: "Does anyone have a reasonable expectation of privacy in respect to this particular sighting?" If the answer is "no," the Fourth Amendment does not apply to the visual observation because it is neither search nor seizure. But for the officer in this hypothetical situation to enter the motel room to seize the evidence, he would have to comply with the Fourth Amendment, using either a warrant or an exception (if one exists) to the warrant requirement. As stated above, the plain view doctrine of warrantless seizure involves several requirements. First, the officer must be lawfully present in the position from which a plain view observation (sighting) is made. Second, the item observed must be "immediately apparent" to be evidence of a crime. "Immediately apparent" means there is, upon sighting, probable cause to believe it is evidence of a crime. If these two requirements are satisfied, the officer may seize the item, provided no further privacy intrusion is required. A further intrusion, for example, would be going from outside a motel room to inside the room. In the motel room scenario above, the officer making the plain view sighting was

The item observed must be "immediately apparent" to be evidence of a crime.

not in a position from which a seizure could be accomplished. An additional intrusion would be necessary to accomplish the seizure. The officer's sighting of items in "plain view" would provide probable cause but would not activate the plain view doctrine of warrantless seizure. The plain view doctrine of warrantless seizure is not legal authority for an officer to enter private premises.

Compare, though, the Supreme Court decision in *Minnesota v. Carter*, 525 U.S. 83 (1998), where an officer looked into an apartment window from outside and saw two men packaging drugs inside. Without addressing whether such an observation into an apartment would ever infringe upon a reasonable expectation of privacy, the Court held that the two temporary visitors, there for illegal commercial purposes, did not have a reasonable privacy expectation in that apartment. Therefore, the Fourth Amendment was not implicated, much less violated, with respect to those two men.

These same principles are operative with respect to entering motor vehicles. For example, consider the frisk of the passenger compartment of a lawfully-stopped vehicle based on reasonable suspicion that weapons are present. During the frisk, should an officer observe a bag of cocaine on the floor board of the car, the officer may utilize the plain view doctrine of warrantless seizure to seize the cocaine. The officer was lawfully present in the vehicle, the cocaine was in plain view, the cocaine was immediately apparent to be evidence of a crime, and no further intrusion was necessary to effect the seizure. However, if an officer standing outside a vehicle parked on a street were to look into the car and see a bag of cocaine on the seat, the officer has made a lawful plain view observation but a further intrusion (going into the car) would be required to accomplish the evidence seizure. That further intrusion would require Fourth Amendment justification beyond the "plain view doctrine." In this case, the "*Carroll* Doctrine" (the vehicle exception to the search warrant requirement) would be available.

Prior to 1990, the Supreme Court had held that the plain view doctrine required an officer's sighting to be "inadvertent."

Prior to 1990, the Supreme Court had held that the plain view doctrine required an officer's sighting to be "inadvertent" – unplanned, unanticipated. In *Horton v. California*, 496 U.S.

128 (1990), the Supreme Court eliminated the inadvertence requirement. Now an officer may use the plain view doctrine of warrantless seizure even when the officer observes items he was fully expecting to see, provided the seizure meets the other requirements of the doctrine.

Now an officer may use the plain view doctrine of warrantless seizure even when the officer observes items he was fully expecting to see, provided the seizure meets the other requirements of the doctrine.

Also important is the Supreme Court decision in *Arizona v. Hicks*, 480 U.S. 321 (1987). In that case, an officer was lawfully present in a home, based on consent. While waiting there, the officer noticed expensive-looking stereo equipment in the otherwise very inexpensive-looking quarters. The officer picked up a stereo item and turned it over in order to record the serial number for comparison to stolen property records. The Court determined that the officer's action was a warrantless search, without probable cause, and not an application of the plain view doctrine. The serial number was not in plain view. The object had to be moved and manipulated in order to see the serial number. Because the serial number had not been exposed to public view, it was within a reasonable expectation of privacy. The officer's intrusion upon that expectation of privacy was therefore a search, in this case unlawful for want of probable cause and a warrant.

Sensory Perceptions

For the most part, visual perceptions have little to do with the plain view doctrine of warrantless seizure. The sense of sight or visual observation is only one of the five sensory perceptions available to an officer. When an officer, during the course of a lawful frisk for weapons, feels an item that is immediately apparent to the officer to be crack cocaine, the officer has used the sensory perception of touch or feel. Although the plain view doctrine of warrantless seizure is not available because an additional intrusion (going into the pocket) is necessary, the sensory (touch) perception may furnish probable cause to arrest and search. *But see* the cases of *Minnesota v. Dickerson*, 508 U.S. 366 (1993) and *Bond v. United States*, 529 U.S. 334 (2002), on when too much manipulation of an item itself becomes a search.

Sensory perceptions often require evaluation of the concept of reasonable expectation of privacy and application of the definition of search. In the *Hicks* case, above, the officer lifted a stereo component to see a part that had not been exposed to public view. That was a "search." The smelling of an odor coming from a building by an officer lawfully present on the exterior is not a search and may establish reasonable suspicion or even probable cause. There is generally no reasonable expectation of privacy regarding odors escaping into the public domain; therefore, smelling such an odor usually is not a search. The Fourth Amendment simply does not apply.

Similarly, most courts hold that the suspicion-less "running" of motor vehicle tag numbers is not a search because there is no reasonable expectation of privacy in heavily-regulated licenses that are exposed to public view. See, for example, *United States v. Ellison*, 462 F.3d 557 (6th Cir. 2006).

Understanding when sensory observations are and are not searches can be difficult.

Understanding when sensory observations are and are not searches can be difficult. Consider an actual trial court decision where an officer received an anonymous tip that an individual was cutting drugs on a table inside a seventh-floor apartment. The window curtains were open. There were no other buildings nearby from which the officer could observe the interior of the suspected apartment so the officer went up a small mountain several miles away, used his binoculars, but could not see much detail. The officer then went to a nearby NASA station and borrowed a high-powered telescope. He returned to the mountain from which he could then clearly see the activities inside the suspected apartment. In fact, the officer could read the title of the paperback novel the suspect was reading at the time. The officer observed drugs, obtained a search warrant and, upon its execution, seized a large quantity of narcotics.

The case hinged on whether the observation from the mountainside with the high-powered telescope was a search regulated by the Fourth Amendment. In this case the Court held that the visual observations aided by the telescope were an illegal search. The residents of this seventh-floor apartment, though the curtains were wide open, had a reasonable expectation of privacy, considering that the only way to see in the windows was to station a high-powered telescope on a mountain several miles away. Therefore, the sensory perception (sight) in this case would be a search requiring prior probable cause and a warrant. Generally, though, should the resident or occupant of a building choose to leave the curtains open although there is a public area or neighboring property from which someone can look into the building through the windows, there would not be reasonable expectation of privacy and such a visual observation from neighboring property would therefore be a "non-search."

Sensory Enhancement Tools

Enhancement tools are those used to increase or improve sensory perceptions and abilities. Examples include magnification and illumination devices like binoculars, telescopes, flashlights and night scopes. Drug and bomb sniffing dogs enhance the ability to detect certain odors. Certain microphones and audio equipment can enhance the ability to hear. Overflight surveillance from aircraft allows sightings that otherwise could not be made.

When determining whether use of a particular enhancement tool is lawful, an officer again must consider the concept of reasonable expectation of privacy.

When determining whether use of a particular enhancement tool is lawful, an officer again must consider the concept of reasonable expectation of privacy. In respect to sight, if an unaided observation from the same location would be allowed, then enhancement tools usually are allowed. However, several questions must be considered:

Are the activities occurring in a public area? For these purposes, a public area includes parking lots, street corners, common areas of apartment complexes, and other locations where no one in particular has a reasonable expectation of privacy. In observing such areas, visual enhancement tools almost always are allowed. Consider the use of the telescope from the mountainside discussed earlier. Had the surveillance been of activity taking place on a street corner, the officer could have used the NASA telescope with no legal problems because there would be no intrusion upon a reasonable expectation of privacy.

Are the activities, though in a private area, knowingly exposed to public view? If yes, generally there is no reasonable expectation of privacy and no Fourth Amendment problems with visual observations.

Does the observation require use of an enhancement device that is especially sophisticated or unusual? If the required enhancement device is uncommon in society, one might have a reasonable expectation of privacy based on the notion that a device of that kind was unlikely to be used. If a device is highly sophisticated and/or almost nobody has it, it might be reasonable to expect that it will not be used. See, for example, *Kyllo v. United States,* 533 U.S. 27 (2001), where the Court found that police use of a thermal imaging device to detect the heat signature of a home, even from off the curtilage, was a search in and of itself. The decision relied significantly on the "uncommonness" of thermal imaging equipment and the fact that it could reveal non-criminal activity.

The more remote and/or unusual the required vantage point, arguably the more reasonable is an expectation of privacy.

Is the vantage point remote or unusual? The more remote and/or unusual the required vantage point, arguably the more reasonable is an expectation of privacy.

Generally, officers should not go onto the curtilage or yard of a private residence in order to gain sensory observations. Going onto a curtilage may be a search in and of itself. It is usually permissible, however, to use walkways that are in common public use. For example, an officer may use a commonly-traveled walkway to reach the front door of a private residence. A visual observation or other sensory perception made while on that walkway usually would not be considered a search, even though it was made from within the curtilage. (See discussion of Open Field and Woods, at page 102. Courts are split on whether taking a drug detection canine to a bedroom door pursuant to another resident's consent is a search. See, for example, *United States v. Brock,* 417 F.3d 692 (7th Cir. 2005) and *compare United States v. Thomas,* 757 F.2d 1359 (1985).

General Notes On Surveillance, Enhancement Tools, And Electronic Eavesdropping

While the law in this is not completely clear or entirely logical, certain generalizations are possible. Binoculars are commonly available, so use of them is generally lawful. Flashlights and night scopes, like binoculars, are lawful in almost all circumstances. Using aircraft to fly over suspect locations to look down into an area generally does not implicate the Fourth Amendment even if sophisticated enhancement tools are used, at least as long as the aircraft remains in lawfully navigable airspace. *See California v. Ciraolo*, 476 U.S. 207 (1986), *Dow Chemical v. United States*, 476 U.S. 227 (1986), and *Florida v. Riley*, 488 U.S. 445 (1989). Use of telescopes may or may not be considered a search, depending on analysis of reasonable expectation of privacy discussed earlier. Use of scent detection canines in public areas is generally permissible. *United States v. Place*, 462 U.S. 696 (1983); *Illinois v. Caballes*, 543 U.S. 405 (2005). Tracking devices (like "beepers") are generally permissible except when used to monitor continued activities inside private premises. In the latter event, a search warrant is needed or the monitoring device must be turned off. *See United States v. Knotts*, 460 U.S. 276 (1983), *United States v. Karo*, 468 U.S. 705 (1984) and *United States v. Garcia*, 474 F.3d 994 (7th Cir. 2007) (GPS technology).

Tracking devices (like "beepers") are generally permissible except when used to monitor continued activities inside private premises...The action necessary to install the transmitter for a tracking device may be a search regulated by the Fourth Amendment.

NOTE: The action necessary to install the transmitter for a tracking device may be a search regulated by the Fourth Amendment. Sliding a transmitter under the bumper of a car parked in a public area is not a search. See Cardwell v. Lewis, 417 U.S. 583 (1974). However, if the car was in an area where privacy is reasonably expected, such as in the driveway of a private residence, the installation action might well be a search requiring a warrant.

Wiretapping, electronic eavesdropping, etc., are generally prohibited under federal law unless state law permits. In those matters, inquiry into state law is essential. Federal law permits the interception of oral or wire communication as long as one party to the conversation consents to monitoring. *Hoffa v. United States*, 385 U.S. 293 (1966); *United States v. Lee*, 359 F.3d 194 (3d Cir. 2004). Some state law varies and requires notification and/or all party consent. The interception of oral communication in which there is a reasonable expectation of privacy is a federal felony.

Summary

The more sophisticated and unusual the enhancement tool(s), the more likely it is that the officer's actions would be considered a search.

Proper analysis of these issues requires evaluation of each individual situation. There are few absolutes. If a visual observation is of activity occurring in an area where no one has a reasonable expectation of privacy, the observation generally would not be a search. If the activity is occurring within an area of reasonable expectation of privacy, visual observations may very well be a search and further consideration is required. Generally, the more remote or unusual the vantage point and the more sophisticated and unusual the enhancement tool(s), the more likely it is that the officer's actions would be considered a search requiring prior probable cause and a warrant.

CHAPTER 11

CONSENT TO SEARCH

Asking for consent to search is in fact asking a person to give up a reasonable expectation of privacy. If a valid consent is obtained, an officer may search the item or area in question without any other Fourth Amendment justification. Because it does not involve an intrusion upon a reasonable expectation of privacy, a "consent search" is really a non-search.

For a consent to be valid it must be voluntary, given without undue coercion or duress.

For a consent to be valid it must be voluntary, given without undue coercion or duress. *Schneckloth v. Bustamonte*, 412 U.S. 218 (1973). Officers may not threaten a person with police action in order to obtain consent to a search. However, a truthful statement like, "If you don't consent, I am going to apply for a search warrant," generally is permitted. *See Bumper v. North Carolina*, 391 U.S. 543 (1968) and *United States v. Garcia*, 890 F.2d 355 (11th Cir. 1989). Stating, "If you don't consent, I'm just going to get a search warrant and search anyway," is generally considered too coercive and invalidates a resulting consent. *See United States v. Boukater*, 409 F.2d 537 (5th Cir. 1969). In one case the officer is stating something to be true that he or she controls – application for a search warrant. In the other, the officer is stating something to be true that is actually controlled by intermediary judicial decision-making – suggesting authority that does not yet exist. Differences are subtle but important.

Deception To Obtain Consent

Undercover work involves constant deception and often results in officers being admitted into private premises where, if the truth were known, they would never have been invited.

Courts, including federal courts, are divided on the questions of what types and degrees of deception are permitted in order for police to facilitate a consent process. Obviously, undercover work involves constant deception and often results in officers being admitted into private premises where, if the truth were known, they would never have been invited. Such scenarios rarely result in legal controversy – courts universally accept such undercover work and its necessary deceptions. "Misplaced confidence" does not violate the Constitution. *Hoffa v. United States*, 385 U.S. 293 (1966), *Lewis v. United States*, 385 U.S. 206 (1966). But what about officers posing as phone company employees going to someone's door and explaining a need to come in the house to check for a system problem? Or posing as gas company employees needing to check inside for hazardous conditions that purportedly represent an emergency threat to the safety of the residents? These are the questions which divide the courts – unfortunately, to the extent that no discernible trend can be identified. Creating a ruse outside private premises to draw occupants outside is generally permitted. False representation of legal authority to search voids a consent, according to *United States v. Escobar*, 389 F.3d 781 (8th Cir. 2004), where officers falsely claimed that a drug dog had alerted to the suspect's property. Most courts agree in regard to false claims of legal authority. Creating a ruse in order to facilitate service of warrant is different, of course, and is generally permitted. See, for example, *United States v. Alejandro*, 368 F.3d 130 (2d Cir. 2004).

Who Can Consent?

In general, a valid consent must be obtained from someone who has a reasonable expectation of privacy in the property to be searched. This means that an officer must reasonably believe that the person who is giving the consent to search has the authority to grant consent over the area or item in question. Usually, this involves common-sense judgments under the totality of the circumstances, but there may be very reasonable mistakes in this area. As long as the mistake is objectively reasonable, a resulting consent is still valid. *Illinois v. Rodriguez*, 497 U.S. 177 (1990).

In a case of huge importance, the Supreme Court decided in 2006 that, where both spouses are present at their home, one purportedly granting consent to enter and search and the other denying consent, the purported consent is invalid and police may not enter based on it. *Georgia v. Randolph*, 547 U.S. 103 (2006). One post-*Randolph* case applies the *Randolph* rule even where the objecting co-habitant is not physically present but is talking to police on the phone. *United States v. Hudspeth*, 459 F.3d 922 (8th Cir. 2006).

Where both spouses are present at their home, one purportedly granting consent to enter and search and the other denying consent, the purported consent is invalid and police may not enter based on it.

Of course, if there is another operative theory that would permit entry and/or search, probable cause plus exigent circumstances for example, those actions would be permitted and are unaffected by the *Randolph* case. Generally, however, either spouse living in a home may consent to search of the areas commonly and mutually used. *See United States v. Matlock*, 415 U.S. 164 (1974) and *United States v. Solis*, 299 F.3d 420 (5th Cir. 2002). Roommate situations are treated much like spouses. In either case, consent by one is invalid as to areas in which another person has exclusive privacy interests.

A parent generally may consent to the search of the bedroom of a child. *See United States v. Rith*, 164 F.3d 1323 (10th Cir. 1999). However, there are situations where such a consent may not be valid. Factors such as the child's age, whether there is regular access by the parent to the room, and/or rent being paid by the child may change things. The "child" could be an adult living in the parent's home. A "child" may reach an age and a status such that he may actually be able to give a valid consent to search the common area of a home (like spouses or roommates). Young children generally cannot validly consent to a search of their parents' home, although there is a federal appeals court decision saying a nine-year old could consent to entry. *Lenz v. Winburn*, 51 F.3d 1540 (11th Cir. 1995). It was crucial in that case that the "consent" only validated the officers' stepping inside the front door to wait for the arrival of an adult. It was not a valid consent to search.

In almost all cases involving landlord-tenant relationships, the consent must be obtained from the tenant, the person with the reasonable expectation of privacy. *See Chapman v. United States*, 365 U.S. 610 (1961). Thus, a landlord generally may not consent to the search of the tenant's residence, even if there is a lease provision that allows him to inspect the property for maintenance or other purposes. *See United States v. Warner*, 843 F.2d 401 (9th Cir. 1988). However, a tenant may consent to a search of the property he rents even over the objections of the landlord.

The overnight house guest who has sole use of a bedroom has a reasonable expectation of privacy in that room.

In overnight house guest situations, the homeowner's consent is required for search of the house in general. However, the overnight house guest who has sole use of a bedroom has a reasonable expectation of privacy in that room. Consent to search that room must be obtained from the house guest. *Minnesota v. Olson*, 495 U.S. 91 (1990).

In an employer-employee situation, consent of the employer is generally adequate for workplace searches; however, employees may have a personal reasonable expectation of privacy in some areas within the workplace. Some employers reduce or eliminate reasonable privacy expectations of employees by notifying them that areas such as lockers, desks, and offices belong to the employer, are subject to inspection at any time, and that lock combinations must be filed with the employer. In such cases, the employer may conduct a "non-search" of an employee's "personal area" because, in fact, the employee does not have a reasonable expectation of privacy in that area. However, the way an area is actually used over a period of time can change the result. See, for example, *O'Connor v. Ortega*, 480 U.S. 709 (1987).

In owner-custodian relationships where the owner leaves an object in the care of another – at a valet-involved parking garage, for example – federal case law is unclear. Relevant questions include whether the custodian appears to have lawful authority to access the areas as to which consent is being requested or his role is just "storage" of the object. "Access authority" makes it more likely a valid consent can be obtained from the custodian, but does not necessarily settle the issue. *See United States v. Basinski*, 226 F.3d 829 (7th Cir. 2000). For insights into who can consent to a search of computer files, see *United States v. Buckner*, 473 F.3d 551 (4th Cir. 2007) and *United States v. Ziegler*, 474 F.3d 1184 (9th Cir. 2007).

Consent Considerations Arising Out Of An Officer's Language

Officers should ask for consent in a way that clearly indicates a real choice, should make their requests clear, and may also wish to define the scope of the search they wish to conduct. When asking to search a vehicle, good words would be: "May I have permission to search you, your vehicle, and its contents?" In that case, there is no question that a consent to search is being requested for the person, the vehicle and the contents of the vehicle, and that the person has a choice.

Officers are not required to advise of the right to refuse consent.

Officers are not required to advise of the right to refuse consent. *United States v. Drayton*, 536 U.S. 194 (2002). However, there may be cases involving mental impairment, age, or other circumstances in which an officer would want to advise a person of his right to refuse so that the consent is strengthened.

A person who has been stopped need not be informed that he is free to leave in order to get a valid consent to a search. In *Ohio v. Robinette*, 519 U.S. 33 (1996), Robinette was stopped for traffic law violation. The officer asked for consent to search after issuing a warning and returning Robinette's drivers license, but without saying "You're free to leave." The resulting consent was valid, according to the Court.

Consents are not required to be in writing. Proving a valid consent requires testimonial credibility, whether or not a form is used. Recording the consent conversation provides better documentation than does a form and is helpful where state law permits.

Officers are not required to describe what they are searching for in order to obtain a valid consent. However, if the officer does not identify small objects of search or request permission to conduct a "complete" search, the scope of the consent could be unclear; a resulting search could exceed the scope of the consent. For a discussion of this issue, *see Florida v. Jimeno*, 500 U.S. 248 (1991). A person in lawful custody may give a valid consent provided no other coerciveness would render the consent involuntary. *See United States v. Watson*, 423 U.S. 411 (1976) and *United States v. Burns*, 298 F.3d 523 (6th Cir. 2002), where a consent from a handcuffed person was found to be valid.

The Consent Itself

A non-verbal gesture may be a sufficient consent under some circumstances.

Officers may wish to clarify any ambiguous response given by the person from whom consent is requested but a non-verbal gesture may be a sufficient consent under some circumstances. *United States v. Drayton*, above. *See also United States v. Carter*, 378 F.3d 584 (6th Cir. 2004) (en banc) for an application of *Drayton*. Consent may be limited. Someone may allow an officer to search a car except for the trunk. He may limit the officer to three minutes searching time. Consent may be given and then revoked. The officer must abide by the limitations placed on the consent unless alternate legal justification exists for a search action.

Consent may be and often should be utilized in conjunction with Fourth Amendment justifications such as probable cause and search warrants. An officer who has probable cause to search a vehicle stopped on a public street may wish to obtain consent to search the vehicle, even though warrantless search is already authorized under another exception to the warrant requirement. A valid consent on top of the alternate search justification simply makes police victory in court more likely. If there is something wrong with the consent, the other justification is still viable, and vice versa.

An officer who has probable cause to search a vehicle stopped on a public street may wish to obtain consent to search the vehicle, even though warrantless search is already authorized under another exception to the warrant requirement.

CHAPTER 12

SEARCH WARRANTS

The law of search warrants is always a combination of federal constitutional principles and state law requirements. State law usually has much to say regarding search warrant application and execution procedures. This discussion focuses on federal constitutional requirements, while noting frequently recurring state law issues.

The law of search warrants is always a combination of federal constitutional principles and state law requirements.

The Fourth Amendment to the United States Constitution states:

> "The right of the people to be secure in their persons, houses, papers, and effects, against unreasonable searches and seizures, shall not be violated; and no warrant shall issue but upon probable cause, supported by oath or affirmation and particularly describing the place to be searched and the persons or things to be seized."

So, the Fourth Amendment requires that:

1. All search and seizures be "reasonable."
2. Warrants be based on "probable cause."
3. Warrants be supported by "oath or affirmation."
4. Warrants "particularly describe" the place to be searched and person or things to be seized.

Exceptions To The Warrant Requirement

As earlier discussed, not every search and/or seizure requires a search warrant. There are a variety of searches that fall within well-established exceptions to the warrant requirement. Examples include frisks, searches incident to arrest, and inventory searches. Certain other police actions do not require a warrant because they are not searches as that term is defined in Fourth Amendment law. Examples include consent "searches," observations in open fields and woods, and certain other observations/perceptions in or of public areas.

The Benefits Of A Warrant

Where the law is unclear as to whether or not a warrantless search is permitted, officers might consider:

1. A search warrant will sometimes permit a more extensive search than would be the case if a warrantless search was conducted.

2. Obtaining a warrant often will help protect an officer from civil liability and/or criminal prosecution.

3. There is a procedural advantage in obtaining a warrant. The criminal defendant has the burden of showing lack of probable cause or other defect when trying to suppress evidence seized pursuant to a warrant. The prosecution has the burden of proving probable cause when searches and seizures are made without a warrant and of proving that the warrantless search was lawful.

4. Evidence seized pursuant to a warrant is sometimes admissible even when it is ultimately determined that probable cause was lacking. Under federal law, there is a partial "good faith" exception to the exclusionary rule when an officer reasonably relies on an apparently valid search warrant. *See Massachusetts v. Sheppard,* 468 U.S. 981 (1984) and *United States v. Leon*, 468 U.S. 897 (1984).

5. "Anticipatory" search warrants – which become effective only upon the occurrence of a triggering event – may be useful occasionally. See, for example, *United States v. Grubbs*, 547 U.S. 90 (2006).

Definitions Of Key Terms

What Is A Search Warrant?

A search warrant is a judicial order. Typically, it commands that a law enforcement officer (with territorial jurisdiction) conduct the search and seizure action(s) authorized by the warrant. A more accurate name for a search warrant would be a "search and seizure warrant" because nearly all search warrants order a seizure.

A more accurate name for a search warrant would be a "search and seizure warrant" because nearly all search warrants order a seizure.

What Is A Seizure?

Generally, a seizure is either a significant governmental interference with someone's possessory interest in property, or the arrest or detention of a person. The thing to be seized, whether an item of property or a person, is almost always the ultimate goal of a search warrant.

What Is A Search?

A search is a governmental intrusion upon a reasonable expectation of privacy. When an officer intrudes upon a reasonable expectation of privacy, a search warrant will be required, unless the action falls within a recognized exception to the search warrant requirement.

What Is Involved In Applying For A Search Warrant?

A search warrant application consists mainly of several descriptions and a probable cause statement. Every jurisdiction publishes forms that guide the application process.

Descriptions

The Fourth Amendment explicitly requires that search warrants particularly describe both the places to be searched and the person(s) and/or thing(s) to be seized.

The Fourth Amendment explicitly requires that search warrants particularly describe both the places to be searched and the person(s) and/or thing(s) to be seized. This is the first major component of a search warrant application. If this requirement is not met, the warrant is constitutionally defective, resulting evidence will usually be suppressed, and liability exposures are created. There are actually three things that must be sufficiently described:

1. The Crime (that is believed to have occurred).
2. The Evidence (that is to be seized).
3. The Place (that is to be searched).

In describing the crime, it is best to use a plain-language reference even if a statute number or some other technical reference is used. That way, if a mistake is made with a number or reference, there will still be a sufficient description of the crime. "Rape" would probably be a sufficient crime description. Adding the degree, type, statute number, or other technical reference bolsters the description and would be helpful to include. Date, place, and victim identifiers might be included as well.

In describing what is to be seized, the effort is to describe the item or person well enough to make it unlikely that the wrong thing or person will be seized. Looser descriptions are accepted when the items to be seized may not be lawfully possessed because all contraband is subject to seizure. So, for example, "cocaine" might be a sufficient description even though there was no description of the variety or packaging. To use such a generic description of an item that may be lawfully possessed (e.g. "television") generally would not be sufficiently particular, and more descriptive information would be required. If known, information should be included as to a person's name, age, race, gender, and as detailed a physical description as is available.

In describing the place to be searched, a rule of thumb should be considered: Describe the place well enough that a person unfamiliar with the case could take the description, go out into the world, and find the right place. Street numbers on houses, for example, are very easy to confuse and/or mistype. A physical description, if available, should be included to minimize the potential for mistake. See, for example, *United States v. Hang Le-Thy Tran*, 433 F.3d 472 (6th Cir. 2006). The same principle would apply to vehicle tag numbers and physical descriptions. If it is known that vehicles and outbuildings are to be included in a search of certain premises, they should be mentioned and described as well as possible. Such a warrant may allow searches of vehicles that arrive after the search has begun. *United States v. Tamari*, 454 F.3d 1259 (11th Cir. 2006). *See United States v. Angelos*, 433 F.3d 738 (10th Cir. 2006) for an example of exceeding the description of the place to be searched.

The Probable Cause Statement

The key to success in writing a probable cause statement is organizing information on paper or electronically before writing out the probable cause statement.

The second major component of a search warrant application is the probable cause statement. The key to success in writing a probable cause statement is organizing information on paper or electronically before writing out the probable cause statement and completing the application. Such an outline or worksheet might start this way:

1. List each item of information by date received.
2. For each item of information, identify the source(s).
3. In respect to each source, state why the source should be believed.

Addressing these issues in writing is the first step toward writing a good probable cause statement. Ultimately, the probable cause statement must link the crime, the place to be searched, and the evidence to be seized by credible information sufficient to form at least a fair probability that the evidence to be seized is in the place to be searched.

Why Should The Information Be Believed?

For purposes of this discussion, "hearsay" is information from a source other than the officer's personal observations. For all hearsay information in a search warrant application, there ideally will be information showing:

1. How the source obtained the information; and
2. Why the hearsay source should be believed.

Prior to *Illinois v. Gates*, 462 U.S. 213 (1983), satisfying this two-prong test was a strict requirement for establishing probable cause on the basis of information supplied by an informant. In *Gates*, the Supreme Court abandoned the requirement that this two-part test be satisfied and held that the informant's reliability and personal basis of knowledge are simply relevant factors to consider when making a probable cause determination. According to *Gates*, probable cause does not depend on a rigid test. Instead, it involves a common-sense judgment based on the "totality of the circumstances." Although satisfying the two-prong test (informant's reliability and basis of knowledge) is no longer strictly required, it remains an extremely valuable drafting technique.

Probable cause does not depend on a rigid test. Instead, it involves a common-sense judgment based on the "totality of the circumstances."

Usually, it is possible to give some reason why a hearsay source should be believed. If the source is a law enforcement officer, that is usually enough. If the source is a regular citizen reporting a crime or an eyewitness, the search warrant application should say things like: "This source is simply a concerned good citizen, is not a paid police informer, is gainfully employed, and has no known reason to lie to police."

If the source is a regular police informant (and a criminal himself), the source's record, if any, of providing accurate information in the past should be recited. If the informant admits participating in the crime, that fact should be included. If the source is paid for accurate information, that should be added.

Corroboration

"Corroboration" is the verification of the accuracy of information received. Corroboration can establish a basis for believing a source of whom little or nothing is known and/or who has no history of providing accurate information. Anything that can be corroborated adds strength to the source's information.

Even an anonymous tip often can be corroborated by checking out the details provided by the tip. Particularly if the anonymous source can predict accurately future events or provide accurate detailed information that requires insider knowledge, there is reason to accord the tipster heightened credibility. See, as examples, *Alabama v. White*, 496 U.S. 325 (1990) and *Illinois v. Gates*, 462 U.S. 213 (1983). If, however, all an anonymous tipster can do is describe a person who is already in a public place – something anyone can do – and then add a conclusory statement of criminal involvement, that is not enough even to establish reasonable suspicion. See, for example, *Florida v. J. L.*, 529 U.S. 266 (2000).

What Is Enough For Probable Cause?

There is no legal formula or scientific test for how much is enough to establish probable cause. Probable cause is ultimately a matter of opinion. As a practical matter, if enough judges agree that the information is sufficient, then there is probable cause. Still, it may help to conceptualize a bit.

Establishing probable cause does not require satisfying a mathematical "more likely than not" standard.

Establishing probable cause does not require satisfying a mathematical "more likely than not" standard. In other words, probable cause may not require a 51% likelihood. It requires more than just reasonable suspicion but may be less demanding than the preponderance, or greater weight, of the evidence. *See Maryland v. Pringle*, 540 U.S. 366 (2003), in which the Court stated that the preponderance of the evidence standard "has no place" in a probable cause determination.

Probable cause admits to the possibility of error. Even at 51% likelihood, the potential for mistake is almost as high as the likelihood of correctness. Probable cause is only a fair probability, not a certainty or proof beyond a reasonable doubt. It is ultimately a common sense judgment made in light of the officer's training and experience and based on the "totality" of the circumstances.

Obtaining The Warrant

When the application form is completed satisfactorily, it may be taken to a neutral, detached judicial official who has authority under state law to issue search warrants. In the presence of that official, the applicant must swear or affirm that the application, often called the "affidavit," is true. If the reviewing official finds the application to be satisfactory, a search warrant (usually on the same form or set of forms) will be issued. Law enforcement officials then must "execute" the warrant.

Search Warrant Execution

While the process of executing a search warrant is partly a matter of state law, certain aspects of the process are fundamental to federal constitutional law.

While the process of executing a search warrant is partly a matter of state law, certain aspects of the process are fundamental to federal constitutional law. For example, the scope of the search must be based on the probable cause and can be no more expansive or intrusive than the probable cause would permit. Otherwise, the search becomes unreasonable and violates the Fourth Amendment. Federal constitutional law also imposes "knock and announce" requirements and "wait times" before entering.

Following are some questions and considerations that should be part of search warrant "execution."

The "Look Right" Test

Does the warrant "look right"? Is the application signed and dated by the applicant and by the issuing judicial official? Does the document contain all its parts? Are all the blocks filled in? Does it look like something is missing? Do the dates make sense? Does the document make sense when you read it? An officer may be held civilly liable for executing an obviously defective warrant. *Groh v. Ramirez*, 540 U.S. 551 (2004).

Jurisdictional Issues

Does the judicial official issuing the warrant have both territorial and subject-matter jurisdiction to issue this warrant? Do the officers who will execute this warrant have both territorial and subject matter jurisdiction to do so? Territorial jurisdiction refers to geographical authority. *Where* does the official have power to act officially? Subject-matter jurisdiction involves whether or not the official has power to act in a matter of the sort in question.

Time Frames

How long is allowed to execute this order? Is this order still valid? States typically have laws that a warrant must be executed within a particular period of time following its issuance. So, police may have to begin (or complete) the search within a prescribed period of time under state law. Some states require that certain kinds of warrants be executed only during certain daylight hours.

Re-Check Of Probable Cause

If probable cause has evaporated, the warrant should not be executed but should be returned to the issuing authority for further instructions.

Has probable cause evaporated? Has the passage of time changed things? Has something new been learned that has caused deterioration of the probable cause? If probable cause has evaporated, the warrant should not be executed but should be returned to the issuing authority for further instructions.

Re-Check Description(s)

What is the scope of the authorized search? Care must be taken not to search areas which are not within the probable cause or that are outside the description of places to be searched under the warrant. What are the items to be seized under the warrant? Seizures of items not described in the warrant may sometimes be lawful under the plain view doctrine of warrantless seizure.

Consideration should include any state law rules regarding items seized while executing a search warrant. For example, the old "inadvertence" requirement in the federal plain view doctrine was eliminated by the Supreme Court in *Horton v. California*, 496 U.S. 128 (1990), but it is possible that a state might have retained the inadvertence requirement in its statutory or state constitutional law. Also, a Supreme Court decision, *Arizona v. Hicks*, 480 U.S. 321 (1987), makes clear that, to seize an item under the plain view doctrine, one must have probable cause to believe that it is evidence of a crime. It is not enough just to suspect that it is. So, if an item is not listed as an item to be seized in the warrant application, and it is going to be seized, there must be probable cause to believe it is evidence of a crime. That probable cause must exist before the seizure occurs.

Knock And Announce Requirements

The Fourth Amendment and most states usually require giving notice of identity and purpose prior to entry.

The Fourth Amendment and most states usually require giving notice of identity and purpose prior to entry. These are commonly referred to as "knock and announce" rules. However, both federal and state law may permit "no knock" entries under certain circumstances. The Fourth Amendment allows a "no knock" entry if the officer has reasonable suspicion that giving notice would:

1. Endanger someone, or
2. Be futile, or
3. Inhibit effective investigation.

See Richards v. Wisconsin, 520 U.S. 385 (1997), *Wilson v. Arkansas*, 514 U.S. 927 (1995), and *Hudson v. Michigan*, 126 S.Ct. 2159 (2006). State law regarding "no knock" entries may be, and often is, more demanding than the Federal Constitution.

Wait Time After Knock And Announce

What is the appropriate "wait time" after the knock and announcement? In some drug cases, a 15- to 20-second wait time is sufficient. *See United States v. Banks*, 540 U.S. 31 (2003). A shorter time than that could be enough under some circumstances. The required "wait time" is not dependent on how long it would take someone to get to the door but rather how long it would take to destroy the evidence sought.

Is There A "Reading" Requirement?

Some state rules require that, after entry, the warrant be read aloud to the person(s) present. In some states, the warrant is read aloud to the premises even if no one except police is present.

"Outside" Assistance

What about "outside" assistance in the execution of the warrant? There are times when a private person could assist dramatically, allowing searches to proceed more quickly, more efficiently, and with less damage. It is best to have specific judicial authorization (in the warrant) if a non-police person is to assist in the search. It is also possible that use of a scent-detection dog could help in searches.

Detaining And Restraining Persons Present During The Execution Of A Warrant

The Supreme Court held in *Michigan v. Summers*, 452 U.S. 692 (1981) that persons present at the scene of a search warrant execution usually may be detained during the search. However, it is possible that, under some circumstances, it would be unreasonable (and unconstitutional) to detain such persons, even if a state statute would permit the detention. Movement within the premises of persons present may be restricted and/or required as reasonably necessary for the safe and effective conduct of the search. See, for example, *Illinois v. McArthur*, 531 U.S. 326 (2001). It is advisable, when possible, to show consideration for personal and/or emotional needs of persons present. In situations where the search is likely to take a great deal of time, special thought should be given to whether or not detention of all persons present is reasonable, and decisions should be made accordingly. In inherently dangerous search warrant executions (involving drug

Persons present at the scene of a search warrant execution usually may be detained during the search.

dealers, weapons, etc.), occupants may be restrained in handcuffs. *Muehler v. Mena*, 544 U.S. 93 (2005).

Protective Sweeps

A protective sweep search presents no legal problems unless it extends to areas that would not be searched anyway under the search warrant.

Thought should be given to the extent and nature of any "protective sweep" that is likely to be required. A protective sweep is a room-to-room clearance of possible threats. A protective sweep search presents no legal problems unless it extends to areas that would not be searched anyway under the search warrant. These questions should arise, and be resolved, when determining the scope of the search under the warrant. Naturally, officers are permitted to take reasonable protective actions as circumstances arise and shift during the execution of the warrant. Reasonable suspicion is the factual justification requirement for protective sweeps of areas that are not already covered by the search warrant or immediately adjacent to the areas covered. *See Maryland v. Buie*, 494 U.S. 325 (1990).

Special Tools And Tactical Teams

To what extent is it appropriate (or not appropriate) to involve a tactical team in the warrant execution? Would a tactical team be "too much" for the circumstances? If a tactical team is utilized, is it prepared to engage in transitional tactics – for example, immediately downscaling the tactics – if upon entry, it is learned that they would be unreasonable? What about the use of diversionary devices and distracters like "flash-bangs," etc? Would they create unreasonable dangers under the circumstances or do clear and present risks justify their use? What about gun-pointing, putting people on the floor, and handcuffing? Will those measures likely be reasonable or might they be excessive given the circumstances?

Persons in a public area may not be automatically frisked just because police are executing a search warrant in the premises.

Searches Of Persons Present

What about searching persons present or who arrive at private premises during the execution of the warrant? A Supreme Court decision, *Ybarra v. Illinois*, 444 U.S. 85 (1979), holds that persons in a public area (a bar, in that case) may not be automatically frisked just because police are executing a search warrant in the premises. Instead, officers must adhere to normal legal requirements for non-consensual frisks – reasonable suspicion of the presence of weapons.

It is advisable to follow the same rule in private premises searches, even though some states have statutory law that purports to allow essentially automatic frisks in such cases. The general rule is that persons present on a private premises are not necessarily subject to frisk and/or full search just because they are on the premises where a search warrant is executed. Any such searches must be carefully conformed to the reasonableness requirement of the Fourth Amendment, even if state statutory law purports to authorize "automatic" searches. Upon entering the premises, a full search of persons present may be conducted if the persons are described as "places" to be searched under the warrant or if there is already probable cause to arrest those persons. In other situations, it is sometimes advisable to postpone the decision as to full search of persons present until the premises search is complete. At that time, it may be easier to determine whether or not there is probable cause to search and/or arrest the persons present and a better decision can be made.

NOTE: The term "full search" used in the above paragraph means the kind of search typically conducted by an officer in a thorough search incident to arrest. It would not usually include strip searches, complete or partial, and would definitely not include body cavity searches except under the most compelling exigent circumstances. Body cavity probes should be conducted only by certified medical personnel.

Media Involvement

In 1999, the Supreme Court decided in two cases that the Fourth Amendment prohibits taking or allowing news media representatives into private premises with a search team. This method of creating publicity is now clearly unconstitutional. *See Hanlon v. Berger*, 526 U.S. 808 (1999) and *Wilson v. Layne*, 526 U.S. 603 (1999). Of course, these holdings do not eliminate the possibility of a voluntary consent from residents/occupants to the media intrusion. In seeking such a consent, police would have to communicate with the residents/occupants very carefully

The Fourth Amendment prohibits taking or allowing news media representatives into private premises with a search team.

in order to avoid coerciveness that could otherwise be present in such a transaction.

Length Of Search

The search pursuant to warrant should be terminated when all items subject to seizure under the warrant have been located or when it has become apparent that a search of reasonable scope and duration will not disclose the items to be seized. In some cases, it may be necessary and/or desirable to seek the issuance of a second warrant so that additional search action may be lawfully conducted.

When leaving the search scene, particularly one that is (or will be, because of arrests) unoccupied, reasonable steps should be taken to assure that the premises are protected and/or secured.

Securing The Premises

When leaving the search scene, particularly one that is (or will be, because of arrests) unoccupied, reasonable steps should be taken to assure that the premises are protected and/or secured. This may sometimes require providing police protection of the premises until repairs can be made or other security measures can be arranged and completed.

Care Of Evidence

Great care should be taken to assure that items seized during the search are protected and accounted for through a strict chain of custody. State law and agency policy should be reviewed to assure compliance with inventory and receipt requirements.

"Return" Of Warrant

Most states and some local jurisdictions have prescribed procedures for the "return" of the warrant, whether or not the warrant is executed and property seized, to the judicial authorities (court) that issued the warrant. Officers should take care to follow applicable state law and/or local procedural rules.

After-Action Reports

Although not usually a legal requirement, a thorough documentation of the activities surrounding search warrant execution is a good idea, both to minimize liability exposure and to further other organizational work – policy making, training, etc.

CHAPTER 13

NON-TESTIMONIAL IDENTIFICATION PROCEDURES

The Fifth Amendment protects people from being compelled to give testimonial evidence against themselves in a criminal proceeding. Non-testimonial identification evidence such as fingerprints, handwriting samples and body fluids, may be taken from suspects under certain circumstances without violating Fifth Amendment rights but may still involve Fourth Amendment rights. This discussion helps answer three questions:

1. What are non-testimonial identification procedures?
2. Which of these procedures are permissible incident to arrest and/or custody?
3. How, if at all, may lawful non-testimonial identification procedures be accomplished out of custody?

What Are Non-Testimonial Identification Procedures?

As the name indicates, non-testimonial identification procedures involve identification evidence other than a subject's own testimony. The retrieval of non-testimonial identification evidence from criminal suspects is vitally important to the successful resolution of many criminal investigations. Oftentimes, a thorough processing of a crime scene and/or victim's body will yield fingerprints, palm prints, footprints, hair, or body fluid evidence. These evidentiary items may be compared later with samples obtained from suspects.

In some investigative scenarios where there are eyewitnesses to a crime, a lineup or show-up (one-on-one identification) involving the suspect may be arranged. In other situations, a suspect's voice may be compared by witnesses to the remembered sound of a perpetrator's voice. A suspect's handwriting may be compared, in some cases, to evidentiary documents containing the perpetrator's handwriting.

The use by police of non-testimonial identification procedures may involve a variety of legal rights which could protect a suspect and create issues for the investigating officer.

The use by police of non-testimonial identification procedures may involve a variety of legal rights which could protect a suspect and create issues for the investigating officer. The violation of a suspect's rights in non-testimonial identification procedures can create civil liability exposure for officers and agencies and can cause the suppression (exclusion) of resulting derivative evidence. These rights could include:

State law rights. Note that state law may be more restrictive/demanding than the federal Constitution. Often, this is particularly so in the case of juvenile suspects.

Fourth Amendment (search and seizure) rights. If non-testimonial identification evidence is derived from an illegal detention, arrest, search, or use of force, the evidence may be excluded from trial consideration. *See Hayes v. Florida*, 470 U.S. 811 (1985), for example. Obviously, civil liability exposure is also present in such circumstances.

Sixth Amendment Right to Counsel (after formal charging). Certain non-testimonial identification procedures require involvement of a defendant's lawyer, if they occur after formal charging (indictment or arraignment) and if the defendant does not waive the right. *Kirby v. Illinois*, 406 U.S. 682 (1972) and *United States v. Wade*, 388 U.S. 218 (1967).

Fourteenth Amendment (due process) rights. Due process of law includes the concept of "fundamental fairness." This would require, for example, that a lineup identification process not be unduly "suggestive" of any particular suspect, i.e., that it be "fair."

Since the retrieval of non-testimonial evidence from suspects does not involve compelled testimony, the Fifth Amendment prohibition against compelled self-incrimination is not implicated by non-testimonial identification procedures. If a person were to voluntarily consent to a non-testimonial identification procedure, the procedure would not implicate the Fourth Amendment.

Non-Testimonial Evidence Gained Through A Search Incident To An Arrest

A lawful, custodial arrest carries with it the authority to retrieve, in a search incident to that arrest, certain non-testimonial evidentiary items from the person of the arrestee. *See Cupp v. Murphy*, 412 U.S. 291 (1973). This non-testimonial evidence may include lineup identification, fingerprints, palm prints,

A lawful, custodial arrest carries with it the authority to retrieve, in a search incident to that arrest, certain non-testimonial evidentiary items from the person of the arrestee.

footprints, photographs, body measurements, head hair samples, fingernail scrapings, and gunshot residue. If a person in arrest custody resists these processes, reasonable force may be utilized to overcome the resistance and recover the desired non-testimonial evidence. Typically, this force would involve utilizing several officers and/or special equipment such as restraints to reduce or eliminate risk of injury to the arrestee. Ideally, it would also involve a court order directing the use of that force reasonably necessary to accomplish the procedure.

Body Searches

Significant bodily intrusions (nonconsensual withdrawal of blood, stomach pumping, and surgical procedures, as examples) typically require a search warrant or similar court order.

Significant bodily intrusions (nonconsensual withdrawal of blood, stomach pumping, and surgical procedures, as examples) typically require a search warrant or similar court order. Occasionally, exigent circumstances may excuse the warrant requirement, such as where there is an immediate need to gather evidence of rapidly changing blood alcohol content of a (reasonably believed) drunk driver after an accident involving serious injuries or fatalities. See, for example, *Schmerber v. California*, 384 U.S. 757 (1966). *See also Winston v. Lee*, 470 U.S. 753 (1985), which involved a minor surgical intrusion to recover a bullet.

Non-Testimonial Identification Orders

A much different situation exists when police do not have probable cause to arrest. It appears that the Federal Constitution permits (as does state law in many states) a court-ordered requirement that a person submit to non-testimonial identification procedures based upon a government showing of reasonable suspicion. In some states that court order is called a "non-testimonial identification order." Even if there is not a statutory procedure in a particular state, a judge or other judicial official could have inherent common law judicial power to issue an order "in the interest of justice" that would permit such a procedure. Such a procedure involves a requirement that a suspect briefly present himself to police or medical personnel for the limited purpose of collecting physical evidence from that person or participating in an identification process.

Usually, states have two criteria built into their statutory procedures for the issuance of a non-testimonial identification order:

1. Probable cause to believe that a crime has been committed; plus
2. Reasonable suspicion that the person (from whom the government seeks to retrieve non-testimonial evidence) committed the crime.

Naturally, there also must be reason to believe the identification process would be useful, given existing evidence, in identifying the perpetrator.

An officer seeking a non-testimonial identification order typically must construct a "reasonable suspicion statement" using the same principles as in drafting a probable cause statement in a search warrant application. The principal difference is that only reasonable suspicion must be demonstrated. Of course, if probable cause were already present, officers could use a search warrant for non-testimonial identification procedures or in some cases simply make an arrest and conduct a search incident to arrest.

Service (Execution) Of Non-Testimonial Identification Orders

Service of a non-testimonial identification order typically does not involve taking the subject into custody.

Because only reasonable suspicion of a person's involvement in a crime has been shown, execution of non-testimonial identification orders differs dramatically from the execution of an arrest warrant. Service of a non-testimonial identification order typically does not involve taking the subject into custody. Instead, it consists only of delivering the court papers and notifying the suspect that he/she must appear at a specific place, usually police or medical facilities, within or at a specified time. The non-testimonial identification order specifies what non-testimonial evidence and/or procedures will be retrieved or conducted. In most states that allow such procedures, a suspect's failure to obey the non-testimonial identification order is contempt of court.

Consent Or Search Warrants

Obtaining a person's consent to the recovery of non-testimonial identification evidence is always an option in lieu of seeking a court order. Seeking a search warrant for the retrieval of non-testimonial identification evidence is also an option if probable cause exists. In such cases, probable cause often would also exist to arrest the suspect for the crime and some non-testimonial evidence might be recovered without a search warrant in a search incident to the custodial arrest.

Juveniles

There are often additional state statutory provisions governing non-testimonial identification procedures involving juveniles.

There are often additional state statutory provisions governing non-testimonial identification procedures involving juveniles. Such statutes are usually more restrictive of police procedure than is federal constitutional law. It is possible that even consensual recovery of non-testimonial identification evidence like fingerprints may be restricted or prohibited under state law regarding juveniles.

Lineups And Photographic Arrays

Lineups involve displaying a suspect's person and/or photograph, along with those of others, to a victim or witness for possible identification of the perpetrator. "Lineups" come in two varieties: Physical lineups involving actual people (sometimes called "corporal" or "body" lineups) and photographic lineups or "arrays."

There is no constitutional requirement that a body lineup or photographic array contain a certain number of participants or photos. Rather, the requirement is simply that the procedure be "fair" – that is, not unduly suggestive. Generally, five or six photographs or persons is adequate. Smaller numbers usually increase the "suggestiveness" of the array.

There are several fundamental principles that reduce suggestiveness in both photographic and physical lineups. The witness or victim should be informed that the perpetrator may or may not be in the lineup and that the witness or victim is under no obligation to identify anyone. The witness or victim should not be informed that he or she has identified the "right" person. Witnesses should not be allowed to collaborate and should view the lineups separately and individually. Of course, the people utilized to form the lineup or array should be somewhat similar in appearance to the suspect.

When Does The Right To Counsel Attach During The Identification Process?

The Sixth Amendment right to counsel "attaches" (comes into play) upon formal charging. After formal charging has occurred, the suspect has a right to counsel at all critical stages of adversary judicial proceedings. A suspect's participation in a physical (body) lineup is considered a "critical stage." *Kirby v. Illinois*, 406 U.S. 682 (1972). The conduct of a photographic lineup or array is not. *See United States v. Ash*, 413 U.S. 300 (1973).

In many states, formal charging is called "arraignment" or "first appearance." Formal charging is generally marked by the first time the defendant appears in court before a judge and prosecutor. The person usually is informed of the charges against him, asked how he pleads, and an inquiry is made concerning appointment of counsel. This signals the initiation of adversary judicial proceedings – the State has committed its resources to prosecute the suspect. Formal charging also has occurred if there has been a grand jury indictment.

The suspect's right to counsel at a physical (body) lineup conducted after formal charging may be waived.

The suspect's right to counsel at a physical (body) lineup conducted after formal charging may be waived. *United States v. Wade*, 388 U.S. 218 (1967). To obtain a waiver, the officer should explain the following to the suspect:

1. He will be placed in a lineup with several other people.
2. A witness will view this lineup in an attempt to identify the perpetrator of a crime.
3. In respect to this lineup he has a right to have a lawyer present to observe the lineup and to advise him.
4. If he cannot afford a lawyer and wants one, one will be appointed to represent him during the lineup.

The officer may then solicit a waiver of rights:

"Do you understand the rights I have explained to you?"

"Do you wish to have an attorney represent you during this lineup?"

Though the right to counsel does not exist prior to formal charging, the presence of the suspect's attorney may quiet later allegations of unfairness and due process violations.

For practical reasons, officers should consider having a lawyer present at lineups even when there have not yet been formal charges. Though the right to counsel does not exist prior to formal charging, the presence of the suspect's attorney may quiet later allegations of unfairness and due process violations.

NOTE: As mentioned, the Sixth Amendment right to counsel applies only to formally-charged matters. If a person has been formally charged in one matter, but a lineup involves a different offense, there usually would be no Sixth Amendment right to counsel in a lineup involving the uncharged matter.

Impermissible Suggestiveness In A Lineup Or Photo Array

An impermissibly suggestive identification procedure may violate the Fourteenth Amendment due process clause, thus creating liability exposures and problems with later in-court identification. Whether the suggestiveness of a procedure is impermissible is judged by a "totality of circumstances" test. *See Stovall v. Denno*, 388 U.S. 293 (1967); *Simmons v. United States*, 390 U.S. 377 (1968); *Neil v. Biggers*, 409 U.S. 188 (1972); and *Manson v. Brathwaite*, 432 U.S. 98 (1977). If the identification procedure is unconstitutionally suggestive, the Court will examine the following factors in deciding whether or not to allow an in-court identification:

1. The quality and length of the original viewing (i.e., at the crime) of the suspect by the eyewitness.
2. The degree of attention shown by the eyewitness at the original viewing.
3. The accuracy of the prior description given by the eyewitness.

4. The percentage of certainty in the identification procedure.

5. The length of time between the crime and the identification procedure. *See Manson v. Brathwaite*, 432 U.S. 98 (1977).

The key question the Court will decide is whether the tainted identification procedure created a substantial risk of misidentification in court. If the answer is "yes," in-court identification would not be permitted. It is quite possible that the answer may be "no," given analysis of the above factor, and that in-court identification may be allowed notwithstanding the impropriety of the earlier identification process.

The key question the Court will decide is whether the tainted identification procedure created a substantial risk of misidentification in court.

Show-Ups

A show-up is display of just one person or photograph to an eyewitness. The witness is simply asked, "Do you recognize this person?" Show-ups should be used very carefully and only soon after a crime occurs (within a few hours, usually). Such procedures, though obviously suggestive, have been approved by the courts because:

1. The victim/witness memory is the best it will ever be.

2. There is a strong need to determine if a detained person is in fact the perpetrator.

3. The suspect is not as likely to have altered his appearance (as he might later) and an appropriate identification may be facilitated.

4. If it is determined that a wrong person has been detained, then that person may be quickly released and search for the actual perpetrator may be swiftly resumed.

See United States v. King, 148 F.3d 968 (8th Cir. 1998), where the United States Court of Appeals noted "quick, on-the-scene identification" is "essential to free innocent suspects and to inform police if further investigation is necessary." Suggestiveness may be reduced somewhat by advising the victim/witness that the subject to be viewed "may or may not" be the perpetrator. A recent case holds that removal or manipulation of a suspect's clothing (e.g. taking off a jacket to display his shirt) to make him look more like the described perpetrator is not impermissible during an investigative detention show-up. *United States v. Askew*, 482 F.3d 532 (D.C. Cir. 2007).

Uncooperativeness

If a person subject to a valid non-testimonial identification court order refuses to cooperate with the procedure, several possibilities exist:

1. The court issuing the order could hold the subject in contempt of court and attempt thereby to force his cooperation.
2. The prosecutor may be able to comment and/or produce evidence in court that the subject was uncooperative, raising the inference of the suspect's guilt.
3. If, given its nature, the identification procedure could be appropriately accomplished by force, a court could order that necessary force be used.

If a person who is in custody refuses to submit to a procedure which reasonably could be completed forcibly, police may use limited force as reasonably necessary to accomplish the procedure.

If a person who is in custody refuses to submit to a procedure which reasonably could be completed forcibly, police may use limited force as reasonably necessary to accomplish the procedure. If it is a body lineup that is refused, police may resort to a photo array. Some have suggested that refusal to participate in a lineup could make a show-up "necessary." In such a conflicted situation, obtaining legal advice and/or judicial guidance would be wise.

CHAPTER 14

THE USE OF FORCE IN POLICE PROCEDURES

The Fourth Amendment Standard Of "Objective Reasonableness"

In *Graham v. Connor*, 490 U.S. 386 (1989), the Supreme Court held that police use of force to seize people who are not already jailed or imprisoned should be analyzed under the Fourth Amendment's "objective reasonableness" standard. Before *Graham*, two leading cases guided use of force analysis and both used "subjective" tests. In *Rochin v. California*, 342 U.S. 165 (1952), the Court concerned itself with behavior that "shocks the conscience." In *Johnson v. Glick*, 481 F.2d 1028 (2d Cir. 1973), the focus was whether the force was applied in a good faith effort to maintain order or sadistically and with malice for the very purpose of causing harm. These cases created tests which turned on the involved officer's state of mind and heart and/or the sensibilities of a particular judge or jury.

Graham erased these comparatively subjective standards and replaced them with one which does not involve subjective inquiries into the law enforcement officer's thoughts, feelings, and motivations. Instead, *Graham* requires examination of only objective circumstances and a "reasonable" officer's response to them.

The *Graham* case began on November 12, 1984, when Dethorne Graham was driven by a friend, William Berry, to a convenience store near Graham's home. Graham quickly entered the store, but immediately left again in a hurried manner. Graham got back into the car with Berry, who quickly drove away. M.S. Connor, a Charlotte police officer, saw all of this. His suspicions aroused, he followed Berry and Graham in his patrol car. Approximately one-half mile from the convenience store, Officer Connor stopped the car containing Berry and Graham to determine what, if anything, had happened at the convenience store.

When Connor approached the car, Berry told Connor that Graham was simply having a "sugar reaction." Connor directed them to wait. After Connor told him he had to wait, Graham got out of Berry's car, running around it twice. Berry asked for Connor's help and, together, they caught Graham and held him, though he was still struggling. In the meantime, four other uniformed Charlotte police officers arrived in response to Officer Connor's request for assistance. They struggled with Graham, before eventually handcuffing him and placing him in a police car. When Officer Connor learned that Graham had committed no crime in the convenience store, police took Graham home and released him. At some point during this contact with police, Graham broke his foot, received cuts on the wrists, bruises on his forehead, and a shoulder injury. He also claimed to have developed a loud ringing in his ear. As bad luck would have it, he was indeed an insulin-dependent diabetic suffering an insulin reaction.

Graham sued the five officers and the City of Charlotte for perceived constitutional rights violations, alleging excessive force in the investigatory stop. The case was tried before a jury. At the close of Graham's case, the trial court directed verdicts for the defendants, using a partly subjective test (pursuant to *Johnson v. Glick*) and finding no evidence of malice or bad faith. An appeal by plaintiff to the United States Court of Appeals for the Fourth Circuit was unsuccessful. Graham then appealed to the Supreme Court, which found that the lower courts had applied an incorrect standard, then set a new one, referring initially to its four-year-old deadly force decision in *Tennessee v. Garner*, 471 U.S. 1 (1985):

> "Today we make explicit what was implicit in *Garner's* analysis, and hold that all claims that law enforcement officers have used excessive force – deadly or not – in the course of an arrest, investigatory stop, or other 'seizure' of a free citizen should be analyzed under the Fourth Amendment and its 'reasonableness' standard, rather than under a 'substantive due process' approach...
>
> "Legal analysis in this area requires careful attention to the facts and circumstances of each particular case, including the severity of the crime at issue, whether the suspect poses an immediate threat to the safety of the officers or others, and whether he is actively resisting arrest or attempting to evade arrest by flight."

"Legal analysis in this area requires careful attention to the facts and circumstances of each particular case."

Adding to the picture, the *Graham* Court continued: "The 'reasonableness' of a particular use of force must be judged from the perspective of a reasonable officer on the scene, rather than with the 20/20 vision of hindsight." Noting that other areas of Fourth Amendment law allow an officer leeway for imperfect decision making, especially given the difficulties of police work, the Court then observed, quoting in part from *Johnson v. Glick*:

"Reasonableness must embody allowance for the fact that police officers are often forced to make split-second judgments ."

> "...with respect to a claim of excessive force, the same standard of reasonableness at the moment applies: 'Not every push or shove, even if it may later seem unnecessary in the peace of a judge's chambers,' violates the Fourth Amendment. The calculus of reasonableness must embody allowance for the fact that police officers are often forced to make split-second judgments – in circumstances that are tense, uncertain, and rapidly evolving – about the amount of force that is necessary in a particular situation.
>
> "As in other Fourth Amendment contexts, however, the 'reasonableness' inquiry in an excessive force case is an objective one: The question is whether the officers' actions are 'objectively reasonable' in light of the facts and circumstances confronting them, without regard to their underlying intent or motivation. An officer's evil intentions will not make a Fourth Amendment violation out of an objectively reasonable use of force; nor will an officer's good intentions make an objectively unreasonable use of force constitutional...The Fourth Amendment inquiry is one of 'objective reasonableness' under the circumstances, and subjective concepts like 'malice' and 'sadism' have no proper place in that inquiry."

Because the District Court and the Court of Appeals erroneously applied a subjective standard, the case was sent back for reconsideration under the newly-prescribed Fourth Amendment standard of objective reasonableness. In the ensuing new trial using the objective standard, police defendants again won, this time in a jury verdict in their favor.

The standard arising from *Graham* is entirely objective – could a reasonable, well-trained officer think it necessary to use a like amount of force under like circumstances? If the answer is "yes," the force is reasonable and therefore constitutional.

Deadly Force

In *Tennessee v. Garner*, 471 U.S. 1 (1985), the Supreme Court established a federal constitutional standard for police use of deadly force to prevent the escape of suspected criminals. The language of the Court's opinion also shed some light on the issue of deadly force used by police in self-defense. According to the Supreme Court, the facts of *Tennessee v. Garner* were as follows.

In Tennessee v. Garner the Supreme Court established a federal constitutional standard for police use of deadly force to prevent the escape of suspected criminals.

At about 10:45 p.m. on October 3, 1974, two Memphis police officers, Hymon and Wright, were dispatched to answer a "prowler inside" call. Upon arriving at the scene they saw a woman standing on her porch and gesturing toward the adjacent house. She told them she had heard glass breaking and that "they" or "someone" was breaking in next door. While Wright radioed the dispatcher to say that they were on the scene, Hymon went behind the house. He heard a door slam and saw someone run across the backyard. The fleeing suspect, Edward Garner, stopped at a six-foot-high chain link fence at the edge of the yard. With the aid of a flashlight, Hymon was able to see Garner's face and hands. He saw no sign of a weapon and, though not certain, was "reasonably sure" that Garner was unarmed. He also thought Garner was 17 or 18 years old and 5'5" or 5'7" tall. (In fact, Garner turned out to be a 15-year-old eighth grader, 5'4", about 100 to 110 pounds.) While Garner was crouched at the base of the fence, Hymon called out "Police, Halt!" and took a few steps toward him. Garner then began to climb over the fence. Convinced that if Garner made it over the fence he would escape, Hymon shot him. Garner was taken by ambulance to a hospital, where he died on the operating table. Ten dollars and a purse taken from the house were found with him.

In using deadly force to prevent the escape, Hymon was acting under authority of a Tennessee statute and pursuant to Police

Department policy, both of which allowed deadly force to prevent escape of at least some felony suspects. The Memphis Police Department's policy was slightly more restrictive than the statute, but still allowed the use of deadly force in cases of burglary. The incident was reviewed by the Memphis Police Firearm's Review Board and presented to a grand jury. Neither took action against Officer Hymon.

When asked at trial why he fired, Hymon basically explained in detail why, had he not fired, the suspect likely would have gotten away. While today many would scoff at such a limited rationale, at the time of the incident much police policy and training embraced state statutory law which in turn reflected the common law "fleeing felon rule" – all of which allowed use of deadly force in such circumstances. The Supreme Court decided to step in.

The issue in the case, according to the Supreme Court, was "the constitutionality of the use of deadly force to prevent the escape of an apparently unarmed suspected felon." The Court held that "such force may not be used unless it is necessary to prevent the escape and the officer has probable cause to believe that the suspect poses a significant threat of death or serious physical injury to the officer or others." As put by the Court:

"It is not better that all felony suspects die than that they escape."

> "The use of deadly force to prevent the escape of all felony suspects, whatever the circumstances, is constitutionally unreasonable. It is not better that all felony suspects die than that they escape. Where the suspect poses no immediate threat to the officer and no threat to others, the harm resulting from failing to apprehend him does not justify the use of deadly force to do so. It is no doubt unfortunate when a suspect who is in sight escapes, but the fact that the police arrive a little late or are a little slower afoot does not always justify killing the suspect. A police officer may not seize an unarmed, nondangerous suspect by shooting him dead...
>
> "Where the officer has probable cause to believe...that the suspect poses a threat of serious physical harm, either to the officer or to others, it is not constitutionally unreasonable to prevent escapes

> by using deadly force. Thus, if the suspect threatens the officer with a weapon or there is probable cause to believe that he has committed a crime involving the infliction or threatened infliction of serious physical harm, deadly force may be used if necessary to prevent escape, and if, where feasible, some warning has been given."

An analysis of the *Garner* opinion is aided by breaking down the immediately preceding paragraph into its subparts:

1. **Life-threatening Escape.** "Where the officer has probable cause to believe that the suspect poses a threat of serious physical harm, either to the officer or others, it is not constitutionally unreasonable to prevent escape by using deadly force." This language focuses on the manner of escape and the threat posed by that escape. If the manner of the escape itself creates an imminent threat of death or serious physical harm to the officer or others, the Fourth Amendment permits deadly force to prevent the escape – without regard to the type of crime originally committed. *See Scott v. Harris*, 127 S.Ct. 1769 (2007), where the United States Supreme Court found a police ramming to end a dangerous high-speed pursuit was reasonable though it created a substantial risk of injury or death to the suspect.

2. **Life-Threatening Felony.** "...if the suspect threatens the officer with a weapon <u>or</u> there is probable cause to believe that he has committed a crime involving the infliction or threatened infliction of serious physical harm, deadly force may be used if necessary to prevent escape, and if, where feasible, some warning has been given." (emphasis added) Here, the language after the disjunctive "or" focuses not on the manner of escape but on the nature of the crime which the suspect has apparently committed. It appears from this language that the Fourth Amendment permits deadly force to prevent escape of certain criminals, even if they are unarmed and non-threatening at the time of their escape efforts. See, for example, *Forrett v. Richardson*, 112 F. 3d 416 (9th Cir. 1997).

The Court created a constitutional requirement that "some warning" be given prior to the use of deadly force "where feasible."

3. **Some Warning Where Feasible.** In the clause analyzed immediately above, the Court created a constitutional require-

ment that "some warning" be given prior to the use of deadly force "where feasible." Because many states do not have such a requirement under their statutes or court decisions, this federal "warning" requirement is an important addition to the law. The absence of this warning, if it was feasible to give it, could make an otherwise constitutional shooting unconstitutional. Presumably, the warning referred to is in the nature of "Police! Stop or I'll shoot!"

4. **If Necessary to Prevent Escape.** These words impose what is known as the "reasonable necessity" rule. In order for deadly force to be constitutionally permissible, there must be probable cause to believe that the use of deadly force is "reasonably necessary" – that if deadly force is not employed, the escape will probably succeed. In some cases, "reasonable necessity" will mean that foot pursuit plus non-deadly force would not likely result in apprehension. In other cases, it will mean that delay in apprehension would create substantial and unreasonable risk to the police or others of death or serious physical injury.

What manner of escape activity will permit deadly force under the constitutional standard?

What manner of escape activity will permit deadly force under the constitutional standard? What types of crimes will, in and of themselves, justify the use of deadly force to prevent escape of the perpetrator? Certainly the use or threatened use of a deadly weapon by the suspect in his escape effort creates constitutional authority to use deadly force to prevent the escape. Hostage-taking and/or life threatening attacks during escape efforts, even by unarmed suspects, would likely permit deadly force. Crimes which would seem to qualify as involving the infliction or threatened infliction of serious physical harm include homicides, armed robberies, and life-threatening felonious assaults, as well as certain forms of kidnapping, arson, and rape. Although the *Garner* case does not make it clear, caution dictates that its rule regarding deadly force to apprehend these certain types of criminals probably should be applied only during the suspect's immediate and continuous flight from the crime scene or area. The use of deadly force to prevent his escape when spotted two weeks or two hours after the crime is highly questionable, at best.

Federal constitutional law permits law enforcement officers to use deadly force to apprehend criminal suspects when there is "probable cause to believe that the suspect poses a threat of serious physical harm...to the officer or to others..." and if deadly force "is necessary" to effect the apprehensions. So two factors – dangerousness and necessity – are relevant to the question whether deadly force is constitutionally permissible.

NOTE: Some state law and most police department policies are considerably more restrictive of deadly force than is the federal constitutional standard.

No Requirement Of Least Intrusive Alternative

Because the *Graham v. Connor* use of force standard has been so helpful to police in civil lawsuits, attorneys representing plaintiffs often challenge officer decision making on peripheral and preceding matters in an effort to make them the focus of constitutional concern. Such claims include:

1. Less intrusive alternatives were available and should have been used; therefore, the force actually used was not reasonable; or

2. The officer made choices and took actions that were not necessary, thereby creating the "necessity" for the use of force.

Fortunately for police, federal appeals courts have established a clearly discernible trend that an officer is not required by the Constitution to use the least intrusive force alternative, only a "reasonable" one. Also, the fact an officer could have made better choices or decisions in the events that preceded the application of force will not render the officer's force response unconstitutional.

An officer is not required by the Constitution to use the least intrusive force alternative, only a "reasonable" one.

In *Cole v. Bone*, 993 F.2d 1328 (8th Cir. 1993), the Eighth Circuit United States Court of Appeals stated: "The Constitution...requires only that the seizure be objectively reasonable, not that the officer pursue the most prudent course of action as judged by 20/20 hindsight." In *Illinois v. Lafayette*, 462 U.S. 640 (1983) (an inventory search case), the Supreme Court held that the Fourth Amendment does not require selection of "the least intrusive alternative, only a reasonable one." In

Plakas v. Drinski, 19 F.3d 1143 (7th Cir. 1994), plaintiffs argued that the officer should have used non-deadly alternatives, such as chemical mace or a canine, to defeat the threat caused by a handcuffed but fireplace poker wielding assailant. The Appellate Court explained:

> "There is no precedent in this Circuit (or any other) which says that the Constitution requires police to use all feasible alternatives to avoid a situation where deadly force can justifiably be used. There are, however, cases which support the assertion that where deadly force is otherwise justified under the Constitution, there is no constitutional duty to use non-deadly alternatives first.
>
> "As [the suspect] moved toward [the officer], was he supposed to think of an attack dog, of…CS gas, of how fast he could run backward? Our answer is, and has been, no, because there is too little time for the officer to do so and too much opportunity to second-guess that officer."

Responding directly to the plaintiff's contention that police should have had and used non-deadly or "less-lethal" force equipment, the Court ruled:

"It is clear that the Constitution does not enact a police administrator's equipment list."

> "There can be reasonable debates about whether the Constitution also enacts a code of criminal procedure, but we think it is clear that the Constitution does not enact a police administrator's equipment list."

Then rejecting the argument that the officer was constitutionally-required to have acted differently in the events preceding the use of force, the Court found that such analysis would "nearly always reveal that something different could have been done if the officer knew the future before it occurred…" and stated:

> "Other than random attacks, all such cases begin with the decision of a police officer to do something, to help, to arrest, to inquire. If the officer had decided to do nothing, then no force would have been used. In this sense, the police officer always causes the trouble. However, it is trouble which the police officer is sworn to cause,

> which society pays him to cause and which, if kept within constitutional limits, society praises the officer for causing."

Likewise in *Scott v. Henrich*, 39 F.3d 912 (9th Cir. 1994), the plaintiff claimed that the officers should have proceeded differently and thereby might have avoided the need for deadly force. The Appellate Court rejected plaintiff's argument and had this to say:

> "Requiring officers to find and choose the least intrusive alternative would require them to exercise superhuman judgment. In the heat of battle with lives potentially in the balance, an officer would not be able to rely on training and common sense to decide what would best accomplish his mission. Instead, he would need to ascertain the least intrusive alternative (an inherently subjective determination) and choose that option and that option only. Imposing such a requirement would inevitably induce tentativeness by officers, and thus deter police from protecting the public and themselves. It would also entangle the courts in endless second-guessing of police decisions made under stress and subject to the exigencies of the moment."

"Requiring officers to find and choose the least intrusive alternative would require them to exercise superhuman judgment."

A more recent adoption of these principles is found in *Scott v. Edinburg*, 346 F.3d 752 (7th Cir. 2003). In that case, the Court noted that federal law protects plaintiffs from constitutional violations, not violations of state law, departmental regulations, or best practices.

Another example of this line of decision-making is *Carter v. Buscher*, 973 F.2d 1328 (7th Cir. 1992). In that case, police created a plan to arrest a man who had contracted to have his wife killed. When the plan was executed, the suspect was able to shoot and kill one officer and wound another before being killed himself. Ironically (in the extreme), the deceased suspect's wife (who was the intended victim of her husband's contract murder plan) then sued police, alleging that they should have planned differently (and better) and thus would not have provoked her husband into firing on police and getting himself shot. The reviewing appeals court first found that "pre-seizure conduct is not subject to Fourth Amendment scrutiny," then held: "Even if [officers] concocted a dubious scheme to bring about [the suspect's] arrest, it is the arrest itself and not the scheme that must be scrutinized for reasonableness under the Fourth Amendment."

No state law (or agency policy) may be more permissive than is the Constitution.

In some states, state law is more restrictive of police authority to use force than is the federal constitutional standard. In others, the state standard may be looser – purporting to allow officers greater authority to use force than would the Constitution – and is therefore unconstitutional. Also possible is a mixture; state law may impose certain rules to which must be added one or more federal constitutional requirements. In any event, the starting point is to understand the federal constitutional standard. It establishes the baseline: No state law (or agency policy) may be more permissive than is the Constitution. Then, officers must consider whether their state law or agency policy creates higher – that is, more restrictive – standards which must be met as well. Of course, in most states, nothing prevents a plaintiff from also bringing a force claim under a state law tort theory alleging (civil) assault, battery, and wrongful death, as examples. Given federal constitutional law in this area, many plaintiffs' attorneys will do just that.

CHAPTER 15

LIST OF CASES

Alabama v. White, 496 U.S. 325 (1990)
Arizona v. Fulminante, 499 U.S. 279 (1991)

Arizona v. Hicks, 480 U.S. 321 (1987)

Arizona v. Roberson, 486 U.S. 146 (1988)

Arkansas v. Sullivan, 532 U.S. 769 (2001)

Beckwith v. United States, 425 U.S. 341 (1976)

Berkemer v. McCarty, 468 U.S. 420 (1984)

BeVier v. Hucal, 806 F.2d 123 (7th Cir. 1986)

Bond v. United States, 529 U.S. 334 (2002)

Brigham City v. Stuart, 126 S.Ct. 1943 (2006)

Bumper v. North Carolina, 391 U.S. 543 (1968)

Burket v. Angelone, 208 F.3d 172 (4th Cir. 2000)

Cady v. Dombrowski, 413 U.S. 433 (1973)

California v. Acevedo, 500 U.S. 565 (1991)

California v. Carney, 471 U.S. 386 (1985)

California v. Ciraolo, 476 U.S. 207 (1986)

California v. Greenwood, 486 U.S. 35 (1988)

California v. Hodari D., 499 U.S. 621 (1991)

California v. Prysock, 453 U.S. 355 (1981)

Cardwell v. Lewis, 417 U.S. 583 (1974)

Carroll v. United States, 45 267 U.S. 132 (1925)

Carter v. Buscher, 973 F.2d 1328 (7th Cir. 1992)

Chapman v. United States, 365 U.S. 610 (1961)

Chavez v. Martinez, 538 U.S. 760 (2003)

Chimel v. California, 395 U.S. 752 (1969)

City of Indianapolis v. Edmond, 531 U.S. 32 (2000)

Cole v. Bone, 993 F.2d 1328 (8th Cir. 1993)

Colorado v. Spring, 479 U.S. 564 (1987)

Coolidge v. New Hampshire, 403 U.S. 443(1971)

Cupp v. Murphy, 412 U.S. 291 (1973)

Daughenbaugh v. City of Tiffin, 150 F.3d 594 (6th Cir. 1998)

Delaware v. Prouse, 440 U.S. 648 (1979)

Devenpeck v. Alford, 543 U.S. 146 (2004)
Dickerson v. United States, 530 U.S. 428 (2000)
Dow Chemical v. United States, 476 U.S.227 (1986)
Draper v. United States, 358 U.S. 307 (1959)
Dunaway v. New York, 442 U.S. 200 (1979)
Edwards v. Arizona, 451 U.S. 477 (1981)
Escobedo v. Illinois, 378 U.S. 478 (1964)
Fellers v. United States, 540 U.S. 519 (2004)
Fisher v. San Jose, 475 F.3d 1049 (9th Cir. 2007)
Flippo v. West Virginia, 528 U.S. 11 (1999)
Florida v. Bostick, 501 U.S. 429 (1991)
Florida v. J. L., 529 U.S. 266 (2000)
Florida v. Jimeno, 500 U.S. 248 (1991)
Florida v. Meyers, 466 U.S. 380 (1984)
Florida v. Riley, 488 U.S. 445 (1989)
Florida v. Royer, 460 U.S. 491 (1983)
Florida v. Wells, 495 U.S. 1 (1990)
Florida v. White, 526 U.S. 559 (1999)
Forrett v. Richardson, 112 F. 3d 416 (9th Cir. 1997)
Frazier v. Cupp, 394 U.S. 731 (1969)
Georgia v. Randolph, 547 U.S. 103 (2006)
Graham v. Connor, 490 U.S. 386 (1989)
Groh v. Ramirez, 540 U.S. 551 (2004)
Guzell v. Hiller, 223 F.3d 518 (7th Cir. 2000)
Hairston v. United States, 905 A.2d 765 (D.C.App. 2006)
Hanlon v. Berger, 526 U.S. 808 (1999)
Hardesty v. Hamburg Township, 461 F.3d 646 (6th Cir. 2006)
Hayes v. Florida, 470 U.S. 811 (1985)
Hester v. United States, 265 U.S. 57 (1924)
Hiibel v. District Court of Nevada, 542 U.S. 177 (2004)
Hoffa v. United States, 385 U.S. 293 (1966)

Horton v. California, 496 U.S. 128 (1990)
Hudson v. Michigan, 126 S.Ct. 2159 (2006)
Illinois v. Caballes, 543 U.S. 405 (2005)
Illinois v. Gates, 462 U.S. 213 (1983)
Illinois v. Lafayette, 462 U.S. 640 (1983)
Illinois v. Lidster, 540 U.S. 419 (2004)
Illinois v. McArthur, 531 U.S. 326 (2001)
Illinois v. Perkins, 496 U.S. 292 (1990)
Illinois v. Rodriguez, 497 U.S. 177 (1990)
Illinois v. Wardlow, 528 U.S. 119 (2000)
INS v. Delgado, 466 U.S. 210 (1984)
Johnson v. Campbell, 332 F.3d 199 (3d Cir. 2003)
Johnson v. Glick, 481 F.2d 1028 (2d Cir. 1973)
Jones v. United States, 362 U.S. 257 (1960)
Katz v. United States, 389 U.S. 347 (1967)
Kaupp v. Texas, 538 U.S. 626 (2003)
Kirby v. Illinois, 406 U.S. 682 (1972)
Kiser v. City of Huron, 219 F.3d 814 (8th Cir. 2000)
Knowles v. Iowa, 525 U.S. 113 (1998)
Kyllo v. United States, 533 U.S. 27 (2001)
Lenz v. Winburn, 51 F.3d 1540 (11th Cir. 1995)
Lewis v. United States, 385 U.S. 206 (1966)
Malley v. Briggs, 475 U.S. 335 (1986)
Manson v. Brathwaite, 432 U.S. 98 (1977)
Maryland v. Buie, 494 U.S. 325 (1990)
Maryland v. Dyson, 527 U.S. 465 (1999)
Maryland v. Pringle, 540 U.S. 366 (2003)
Maryland v. Wilson, 519 U.S. 408 (1997)
Massachusetts v. Sheppard, 468 U.S. 981 (1984)
McCalvin v. Yukins, 444 F.3d 713 (6th Cir. 2006)
McClish v. Nugent, 2007 WL 1063337 (11th Cir. 2007)
McConney v. City of Houston, 863 F.2d 1180 (5th Cir. 1989)

McNeil v. Wisconsin, 501 U.S. 171 (1991)
Michigan v. Jackson, 475 U.S. 625 (1986)
Michigan v. Long, 463 U.S. 1032 (1983)
Michigan v. Mosley, 423 U.S. 96 (1975)
Michigan v. Summers, 452 U.S. 692 (1981)
Michigan v. Thomas, 458 U.S. 259 (1982)
Michigan v. Tyler, 436 U.S. 499 (1978)
Mincey v. Arizona, 437 U.S. 385 (1978)
Minnesota v. Carter, 525 U.S. 83 (1998)
Minnesota v. Dickerson, 508 U.S. 366 (1993)
Minnesota v. Olson, 495 U.S. 91 (1990)
Minnick v. Mississippi, 498 U.S. 146 (1990)
Miranda v. Arizona, 384 U.S. 436 (1966)
Missouri v. Seibert, 542 U.S. 600 (2004)
Muehler v. Mena, 544 U.S. 93 (2005)
Neil v. Biggers, 409 U.S. 188 (1972)
New York v. Belton, 453 U.S. 454 (1981)
New York v. Class, 475 U.S. 106 (1986)
New York v. Quarles, 467 U.S. 649 (1984)
North Carolina v. Butler, 441 U.S. 369 (1979)
O'Connor v. Ortega, 480 U.S. 709 (1987)
Ohio v. Robinette, 519 U.S. 33(1996)
Oliver v. United States, 466 U.S. 170 (1984)
Oregon v. Elstad, 470 U.S. 298 (1985)
Oregon v. Mathiason, 429 U.S. 492 (1977)
Park v. Shiflett, 250 F.3d 843 (4th Cir. 2001)
Patterson v. Illinois, 487 U.S. 285 (1988)
Paulino v. Castro, 371 F.3d 1083 (9th Cir. 2004)
Payton v. New York, 445 U.S. 573 (1980)
Pennsylvania v. Bruder, 488 U.S. 9 (1988)
Pennsylvania v. Labron, 518 U.S. 938 (1996)
Pennsylvania v. Mimms, 434 U.S. 106 (1977)

Pennsylvania v. Muniz, 496 U.S. 582 (1990)

Plakas v. Drinski, 19 F.3d 1143 (7th Cir. 1994)

Rawlings v. Kentucky, 448 U.S. 98 (1980)

Rhode Island v. Innis, 446 U.S. 291 (1980)

Richards v. Wisconsin, 520 U.S. 385 (1997)

Rochin v. California, 342 U.S. 165 (1952)

Rosa v. McCray, 396 F.3d 210 (2d Cir. 2005)

Roviaro v. United States, 353 U.S. 53 (1957)

Schmerber v. California, 384 U.S. 757 (1966)

Schneckloth v. Bustamonte, 412 U.S. 218 (1973)

Scott v. Edinburg, 346 F.3d 752 (7th Cir. 2003)

Scott v. Harris, 127 S.Ct. 1769 (2007)

Scott v. Henrich, 39 F.3d 912 (9th Cir. 1994)

Simmons v. United States, 390 U.S. 377 (1968)

South Dakota v. Opperman, 428 U.S. 364 (1976)

Stansbury v. California, 511 U.S. 318 (1994)

Steagald v. United States, 451 U.S. 204 (1981)

Tennessee v. Garner, 471 U.S. 1 (1985)

Terry v. Ohio, 392 U.S. 1 (1968)

Texas v. Cobb, 532 U.S. 162 (2001)

Thompson v. Olson, 798 F.2d 552 (1st Cir. 1986)

Thornton v. United States, 540 U.S. 1102 (2004)

Thornton v. United States, 541 U.S. 615 (2004)

United States v. $109,179 in U.S. Currency, 228 F.3d 1080 (9th Cir. 2000)

United States v. Acosta-Colon, 157 F.3d 9 (1st Cir. 1998)

United States v. Al Nasser, 479 F.3d 1166 (9th Cir. 2007)

United States v. Alejandro, 368 F.3d 130 (2d Cir. 2004)

United States v. Angelos, 433 F.3d 738 (10th Cir. 2006)

United States v. Arnold, 388 F.3d 237 (7th Cir. 2004)

United States v. Arvizu, 534 U.S. 266 (2002)

United States v. Ash, 413 U.S. 300 (1973)

United States v. Askew, 482 F.3d 532 (D.C. Cir. 2007)

United States v. Avila-Dominguez, 610 F.2d 1266 (1980)

United States v. Banks, 540 U.S.31 (2003)

United States v. Banshee, 91 F.3d 99 (11th Cir. 1996)

United States v. Barajas- Avalos, 359 F.3d 1204 (9th Cir. 2004)

United States v. Barboza, 412 F.3d 15 (1st Cir. 2005)

United States v. Barnes, 195 F.3d 1027 (8th Cir. 1999)

United States v. Basinski, 226 F.3d 829 (7th Cir. 2000)

United States v. Bishop, 264 F.3d 919 (9th Cir. 2001)

United States v. Bonner, 263 F.3d 213 (3d Cir. 2004)

United States v. Boukater, 409 F.2d 537 (5th Cir. 1969)

United States v. Bowman, 215 F.3d 951 (9th Cir. 2000)

United States v. Bradley, 321 F.3d 1212 (9th Cir. 2003)

United States v. Brock, 417 F.3d 692 (7th Cir. 2005)

United States v. Buckner, 473 F.3d 551 (4th Cir. 2007)

United States v. Burns, 298 F.3d 523 (6th Cir. 2002)

United States v. Bustos-Torres, 396 F.3d 935 (8th Cir. 2005)

United States v. Carter, 378 F.3d 584 (6th Cir. 2004)

United States v. Cash, 378 F.3d 745 (8th Cir. 2004)

United States v. Chambers, 395 F.3d 563 (6th Cir. 2005)

United States v. Chauncey, 420 F.3d 864 (8th Cir. 2005)

United States v. Clayton, 210 F.3d 841 (8th Cir. 2000)

United States v. Codd, 956 F.2d 1109 (11th Cir. 1992)

United States v. Coles, 437 F.3d 361 (3d Cir. 2006)

United States v. Colon, 250 F.3d 130 (2d Cir. 2001)

United States v. Cordova, 990 F.2d 1035 (8th Cir. 1993)

United States v. Cortez, 449 U.S. 411 (1981)

United States v. Crapser, 472 F.3d 1141 (9th Cir. 2007)

United States v. Currence, 446 F.3d 554 (4th Cir. 2006)

United States v. Delfin-Colima, 464 F.3d 392 (3d Cir. 2006)

United States v. Dorais, 241 F.3d 1124 (9th Cir. 2001)

United States v. Drayton, 536 U.S. 194 (2002)

United States v. Dunn, 480 U.S. 294 (1987)

United States v. Edwards, 415 U.S. 800 (1975)

United States v. Elder, 466 F.3d 1090 (7th Cir. 2006)

United States v. Ellison, 462 F.3d 557 (6th Cir. 2006)

United States v. Escobar, 389 F.3d 781 (8th Cir. 2004)

United States v. Felix-Felix, 275 F.3d 627 (7th Cir. 2001)

United States v. Fellers, 397 F.3d 1090 (8th Cir. 2005)

United States v. Fiasconaro, 315 F.3d 28 (1st Cir. 2002)

United States v. French, 291 F.3d 945 (7th Cir. 2002)

United States v. Garcia, 474 F.3d 994 (7th Cir. 2007)

United States v. Garcia, 890 F.2d 355 (11th Cir. 1989)

United States v. Garrido-Santana, 360 F.3d 565 (6th Cir. 2004)

United States v. Garzon, 119 F.3d 1446 (10th Cir. 1997)

United States v. Gaston, 357 F.3d 77 (D.C. Cir. 2004)

United States v. Gell-Iren, 146 F.3d 827 (10th Cir. 1998)

United States v. Gil, 204 F.3d 1347 (11th Cir. 2000)

United States v. Gillis, 358 F.3d 386 (6th Cir. 2004)

United States v. Gonzalez-Lauzan, 437 F.3d 1128 (11th Cir. 2006)

United States v. Gorman, 314 F.3d 1105 (9th Cir. 2002)

United States v. Gould, 364 F.3d 578 (5th Cir. 2004)

United States v. Grubbs, 547 U.S. 90 (2006)

United States v. Guerrero-Espinoza, 462 F.3d 1302 (10th Cir. 2006)

United States v. Hang Le-Thy Tran, 433 F.3d 472 (6th Cir. 2006)

United States v. Harris, 403 U.S. 573 (1971)

United States v. Heath, 259 F.3d 522 (6th Cir. 2001)

United States v. Henry, 447 U.S. 264 (1980)

United States v. Hoey, 983 F.2d 890 (8th Cir. 1993)

United States v. Hrasky, 453 F.3d 1099 (8th Cir. 2006)

United States v. Hudspeth, 459 F.3d 922 (8th Cir. 2006)
United States v. Huffman, 461 F.3d 777 (6th Cir. 2006)
United States v. Humphries, 372 F.3d 653 (4th Cir. 2004)
United States v. Jackson, 415 F.3d 88 (D.C. Cir. 2005)
United States v. Jacobsen, 466 U.S.109 (1984)
United States v. Johns, 469 U.S. 478 (1985)
United States v. Jones, 471 F.3d 868 (8th Cir. 2006)
United States v. Karo, 468 U.S. 705 (1984)
United States v. King, 148 F.3d 968 (8th Cir. 1998)
United States v. Kitchens, 114 F.3d 29 (4th Cir. 1997)
United States v. Knotts, 460 U.S. 276 (1983)
United States v. Lee, 359 F.3d 194(3d Cir. 2004)
United States v. Lee, 413 F.3d 622 (7th Cir. 2005)
United States v. Leon, 468 U.S. 897 (1984)
United States v. Lindsey, 482 F.3d 1285 (11th Cir. 2007)
United States v. Liu, 180 F.3d 957 (8th Cir. 1999)
United States v. Long, 464 F.3d 569 (6th Cir. 2006)
United States v. Lopez, 437 F.3d 1059 (10th Cir. 2006)
United States v. Martinez, 358 F.3d 1005 (8th Cir. 2004)
United States v. Martins, 413 F.3d 139 (1st Cir. 2005)
United States v. Matlock, 415 U.S. 164 (1974)
United States v. Mayo, 361 F.3d 802 (4th Cir. 2004)
United States v. Mayo, 394 F.3d 1271 (9th Cir. 2005)
United States v. McCargo, 464 F.3d 192 (2d Cir. 2006)
United States v. McCarthy, 77 F.3d 522 (1st Cir. 1996)
United States v. McGough, 412 F.3d 1232 (11th Cir. 2005)
United States v. McKoy, 428 F.3d 38 (1st Cir. 2005)
United States v. Mendez, 476 F.3d 1077 (9th Cir. 2007)
United States v. Miller, 430 F.3d 93 (2d Cir. 2005)
United States v. Moran-Vargas, 376 F.3d 112 (2d Cir. 2004)
United States v. Musa, 401 F.3d 1208 (10th Cir. 2005)
United States v. Najar, 451 F.3d 710 (10th Cir. 2006)

United States v. Newton, 369 F.3d 659 (2d Cir. 2004)

United States v. Ojeda-Ramos, 455 F.3d 1178 (10th Cir. 2006)

United States v. Patane, 542 U.S. 630 (2004)

United States v. Pennington, 287 F.3d 739 (8th Cir. 2002)

United States v. Petty, 367 F.3d 1009 (8th Cir. 2004)

United States v. Place, 462 U.S. 696 (1983)

United States v. Powell, 2007 WL 1119641 (D.C. Cir. 2007)

United States v. Pratt, 355 F.3d 1119 (8th Cir. 2004)

United States v. Pruden, 398 F.3d 241(3d Cir. 2005)

United States v. Quezada, 448 F.3d 1005 (8th Cir. 2006)

United States v. Ramirez, 145 F.3d 345 (5th Cir. 1998)

United States v. Reyes, 353 F.3d 148 (2d Cir. 2003)

United States v. Rhind, 289 F.3d 690 (11th Cir. 2002)

United States v. Rhodes, 779 F.2d 1019 (4th Cir. 1985)

United States v. Richardson, 385 F.3d 625 (6th Cir. 2004)

United States v. Riley, 351 F.3d 1265 (D.C. Cir. 2003)

United States v. Rith, 164 F.3d 1323 (10th Cir. 1999)

United States v. Robinson, 414 U.S. 218 (1973)

United States v. Romero, 452 F.3d 610 (6th Cir. 2006)

United States v. Rosborough, 366 F.3d 1145 (10th Cir. 2004)

United States v. Rousseau, 257 F.3d 925 (9th Cir. 2001)

United States v. Rubin, 474 F.2d 262 (3d Cir. 1973)

United States v. Ruiz-Estrada, 312 F.3d 398 (8th Cir. 2002)

United States v. Sanders, 130 F.3d 1316 (8th Cir. 1997)

United States v. Sandoval-Venegas, 292 F.3d 1101 (9th Cir. 2002)

United States v. Santana, 427 U.S. 38 (1976)

United States v. Segura-Baltazar, 448 F.3d 1281 (11th Cir. 2006)

United States v. Sharpe, 470 U.S. 675 (1985)

United States v. Shaw, 464 F.3d 615 (6th Cir. 2006)

United States v. Sidwell, 440 F.3d 865 (7th Cir. 2006)

United States v. Smith, 389 F.3d 944 (9th Cir. 2004)

United States v. Sokolow, 490 U.S. 1 (1981)

United States v. Solis, 299 F.3d 420 (5th Cir. 2002)

United States v. Soto-Cervantes, 138 F.3d 1319 (10th Cir. 1998)

United States v. Stewart, 213 Fed.Appx. 898 (11th Cir. 2007)

United States v. Tamari, 454 F.3d 1259 (11th Cir. 2006)

United States v. Thomas, 429 F.3d 282 (D.C. Cir. 2005)

United States v. Thomas, 447 F.3d 1191 (9th Cir. 2006)

United States v. Thomas, 757 F.2d 1359 (1985)

United States v. Vega, 221 F.3d 789 (5th Cir. 2000)

United States v. Ventresca, 380 U.S. 102 (1965)

United States v. Wade, 388 U.S. 218 (1967)

United States v. Warner, 843 F.2d 401 (9th Cir. 1988)

United States v. Williams, 359 F.3d 1019 (8th Cir. 2004)

United States v. Williams, 962 F.2d 1218 (6th Cir. 1992)

United States v. Yang, 286 F.3d 940 (7th Cir. 2002)

United States v. Ziegler, 474 F.3d 1184 (9th Cir. 2007)

Washington v. Chrisman, 455 U.S. 1 (1982)

Way v. County of Ventura, 445 F.3d 1157 (9th Cir. 2006)

Welsh v. Wisconsin, 466 U.S. 740 (1984)

Whitely v. Warden, Wyoming State Penitentiary, 401 U.S. 560 (1971)

Whren v. United States, 517 U.S. 806 (1996)

Wilson v. Arkansas, 514 U.S. 927 (1995)

Wilson v. Layne, 526 U.S. 603 (1999)

Winston v. Lee, 470 U.S. 753 (1985)

Wyoming v. Houghton, 526 U.S. 295 (1999)

Yarborough v. Alverado, 541 U.S. 652 (2004)

Ybarra v. Illinois, 444 U.S. 85 (1979)

INDEX

F

G

H

I

J

K

L

M

N

O

P

R

S

T

U

V

W